POETRY R

SUMMER 2000 VOLUM
EDITOR PETER
ASSISTANT EDITOR STE
ADVERTISING LISA

CONTENTS

The International Brigade
pages 3 – 69

Editorial; John Kinsella on International Poetry Space (4), poems by John Kinsella (7); Philip Salom on his routes to poetry (9); poems by Jane Yeh (12), István Vörös (13), Tom French (15), Adam Schwartzman (16), Monica Youn (18), Sarah Wardle (19), Brian Henry (20); Andrew Osborn on Mark Levine (22); poems by Mary Jo Bang (24), Tracy Ryan (25), Malinda Markham (27), Claudia Rankine (28); Sharon Mesmer on Tom Devaney, Kim Lyons and Edwin Torres (30); Stephen Burt on the century's short poems (33); poems by Stephen Burt (37), Anthony Lawrence (39); Jules Mann on New American Poetry (40); Dennis O'Driscoll on Robert Hass's classic poem (42); Robert Crawford on cosmopolibackofbeyondism (43); poems by Kathleen Stewart (45), Jeff Clark (47), Ellen Hinsey (49); Justin Quinn takes a second look at Wallace Stevens (52); Dennis O'Driscoll on Mark Halliday (54); poems by Mark Halliday (55), Karen Volkman (58); Roddy Lumsden on Stephen Burt and Brian Henry (59); Rod Mengham on Billy Collins (61); poem by Susan Wicks (62); Karen Volkman on new American women poets (63); poems by David Berman (64), John Stammers (67)

The Review Pages
70 – 77

David Wheatley on Jamie McKendrick; Caitriona O'Reilly on Thomas Lynch (71); Sarah Wardle on Roddy Lumsden (73); Ian McMillan on Jim Burns (74); Stephen Burt on Thom Gunn (75); John Greening on Elton Glaser

Poems
78 – 93

by James Tate, Brian Jones (79), Fred D'Aguiar (82), Kate Clanchy (87), Joe Sheerin, Carole Satyamurti (88), Billy Collins (90), Moniza Alvi (91), August Kleinzahler (92)

Reviews
94 – 99

Hugh Macpherson on Charles Tomlinson, James Sutherland-Smith, Alan Jenkins, Matthew Sweeney and György Petri; Ruth Padel on Elaine Feinstein (97)

Poems
100 – 106

by Jane Holland, Tony Roberts (101), Peter Redgrove (102), John Hartley Williams (103), Merryn Williams (104), Hugh Macpherson (105), Tony Curtis (106)

National Poetry Competition
107 – 109

Winning poems from the 1999 competition by Simon Rae, Enda Wyley and Sue Hubbard

Endstops
110 – 112

News, comment, letters

Gerald Mangan is on holiday.

LONDON MAGAZINE

FICTION * MEMOIRS * CRITICISM *
POETRY CINEMA * ARCHITECTURE *
PHOTOGRAPHY * THEATRE * ART * MUSIC

'A fantastic magazine whose place in the history of 20th century literary life grows ever more secure and significant' – *William Boyd, Evening Standard*
Each issue contains over 50 pages of poems and reviews of poetry.

NEW LME POETRY

Herbert Lomas *A Hopeless Passion*
Ted Walker *Mangoes on the Moon*
Robert Conquest *Demons Don't*
Nikos Kavvadias *Wireless Operator*
Patty Scholten *Elephants in Love*
Three Finnish Poets, £7.95 each

Soon and recently in London Magazine
Tom Pickard on Morden Tower
Poems by Pablo Neruda
Michael O'Neill on Douglas Dunn
Peter Carpenter on Thom Gunn and Jamie McKendrick
Subscriptions:
£28.50 p.a. (six issues) to 30 Thurloe Place, London SW7

Single copies £5.99 from discriminating bookshops

POETRY REVIEW
SUBSCRIPTIONS
Four issues including postage:

UK individuals £27
Overseas individuals £35
(all overseas delivery is by airmail)
USA individuals $56

Libraries, schools and institutions:
UK £35
Overseas £42
USA $66

Single issue £6.95 + 50p p&p (UK)

Sterling and US dollar payments only. Eurocheques, Visa and Mastercard payments are acceptable.

Bookshop distribution:
Signature
Telephone 0161 834 8767

Design by Philip Lewis
Cover by Stephen Troussé

Typeset by Poetry Review.

Printed by Grillford Ltd at
26 Peverel Drive, Bletchley,
Milton Keynes MK1 1QZ
Telephone: 01908 644123

POETRY REVIEW is the magazine of the Poetry Society. It is published quarterly and issued free to members of the Poetry Society. Poetry Review considers submissions from non-members and members alike. To ensure reply submissions must be accompanied by an SAE or adequate International Reply coupons: Poetry Review accepts no responsibility for contributions that are not reply paid.

Founded 24 February 1909
Charity Commissioners No: 303334
© 2000

EDITORIAL AND BUSINESS ADDRESS:
22 BETTERTON STREET, LONDON WC2H 9BU

telephone   020 7420 9880   fax 020 7240 4818
email   poetryreview@poetrysoc.com ISBN 1 900771 21 7
website   http://www.poetrysoc.com   ISSN 0032 2156

The Poetry Society is supported by BT

THE INTERNATIONAL BRIGADE

by Peter Forbes

NEW POETS ALWAYS used to emerge from a local context. They would cluster around a magazine, a workshop, or a town like Huddersfield in which the poetry scene had suddenly taken off. Eventually the best poets would break though into national publication and, after about 20 years if they were very good, they might start to be noticed internationally.

But in the age of the net this protracted process isn't really necessary; the new global reality is what Robert Crawford calls "Cosmopolibackofbeyondism", in which the valley cheese is "local but prized elsewhere". Young poets have always travelled, carrying spores of indigenous poetry cultures about the globe and in recent years this peripatetic tendency has reached a new peak. A few magazines, such as *Metre* (based mainly in Ireland), *Verse* (originally based in Scotland but now American), *Salt* (Australian but based in Cambridge), *Thumbscrew* (based in Oxford but with American connections) have published newish poets from a wide range of locations. These magazines share many contributors and most of them have featured in *Poetry Review* in the last five years. When Brian Henry's book *Astronaut* appeared from Arc this year it seemed to mark a consolidation of this movement. Henry is a young American poet, an editor of *Verse*, who has worked in Australia, and this first collection was published in the UK by an Australian editor, John Kinsella, now permanently resident in England.

Because of the nature of this movement, in planning this issue we decided to invite half a dozen poet-editors in Britain, Ireland, the USA and Australia to commission up to three poets and a prose piece that would reflect the burgeoning world-wide English language poetry scene. We were not too rigid about the English-language stipulation: David Wheatley chose a Hungarian as one of his three poets. The editors and their chosen poets are: Stephen Burt (Monica Youn, Adam Schwartzman, August Kleinzahler – the latter not a new poet but co-editors were allowed to put enthusiasm ahead of narrow entry criteria); David Wheatley (Tom French, István Vörös, Jane Yeh); Tracy Ryan (Kathleen Stewart); Karen Volkman (Jeff Clark, Malinda Markham, Claudia Rankine); Dennis O'Driscoll (Ellen Hinsey); Stephen Troussé (David Berman, John Stammers). In some cases co-editors also commissioned prose or a review: Stephen Burt (Andrew Osborn on Mark Levine); Stephen Troussé (Roddy Lumsden on Stephen Burt and Brian Henry); Karen Volkman (Sharon Mesmer on poets from the Poetry Project in New York); Tracy Ryan (Philip Salom on his own poetry odyssey); David Wheatley (Caitriona O'Reilly on Thomas Lynch).

Stylistically the poets selected here demonstrate a rapprochement between formerly warring factions. The American poets tend to have L=A=N=G=U=A=G=E poetry sympathies (what Stephen Burt has called the Elliptical school), or to derive to some degree from the New York School and poets such as James Tate and Stephen Dobyns, whilst remaining in touch with the mainstream. David Berman, interestingly, seems to have some of the characteristics of both Billy Collins – marvels of the quotidian, gentle essayish playfulness – and Mark Halliday – fiercer, more surreal. There is no trace of the New Formalism in these poets (remember that?). Justin Quinn's piece on Wallace Stevens and his reception in Britain and Ireland helps us to understand why these young American poets are so different to their British and Irish peers.

The Australian poets – Kathleen Stewart, Anthony Lawrence, Tracy Ryan, John Kinsella himself – are harder to characterise, but they are closer to American practice than to British modes.

Roddy Lumsden's review of Stephen Burt and Brian Henry (p.59) suggests that the traffic will be two-way from now on. Welcome to the New World Poetry Order.

Geography is History?

JOHN KINSELLA ON INTERNATIONAL POETRY SPACE

PERTH, THE CAPITAL of Western Australia, was, and probably still is, the most isolated capital city in the world. When I lived in Geraldton, completing the last three years of high school, the town's population edged over the rubicon that would make it a city (25 000) – bringing a consciousness of being some kind of centre within the international language of place: district, suburb, town, city, state, country. Whether I was in the country, or in the coastal town/city of Geraldton, or in Perth, I felt isolated. I read science fiction to break down that isolation. I read "great" literature from all over the world. I leapt into computers when they first arrived on the scene, in fact being, so I'm told, the first school child to ever use a computer in a school in Western Australia, possibly Australia. I helped set it up – a Wang PDP 9. It required punch cards of course, and that was a language that escaped the limitations of text and yet created new limitations. Communication fascinated me. It meant freedom, escape, knowledge. At one stage I was communicating by letter with up to 200 poets and writers from around the world – simply so I could feel part of the world. As soon as I was old enough to travel, I did so. In some ways being away from "home" has clarified things for me. Distance does this. From an early age, poetry had meant this to me – metaphor was an alternative reality, a virtual space before the language of technology had provided the terminologies. In the simulacrum I travelled.

Writing poetry was one way of accessing a "universal" space, a global language. The way poetry was presented to readers also fascinated me. I tried to start my first serious literary journal when I was about twenty – it was to be called *Canti*. I collected some excellent material for it, with strong support from that Australian internationalist David Brooks, but a lack of finances defeated me in the end. At the end of the '80s when I founded *Salt* – first issue early 1990 – it was with the same "internationalist" take on things. My influences were as diverse as *New Poetry* (edited by Robert Adamson) and *The Paris Review*. Early issues of *Salt* were fairly well landlocked, but as *Salt* developed so did its international content. It is now a truly international journal. *Salt* is, however, a symptom and not a cause, as indeed is the internationalist angle I bring to publishing material in *Stand* with Michael Hulse (a long time internationalist – also in his capacity as my predecessor at Arc), my role as International Editor at *Kenyon Review*, and International Editor for Arc publications. At the core of it is a desire to cross boundaries, to open up lines of communication. This is not done randomly, but within a code of respect for the integrity of regional concerns and demarcations. For an internationalist, there are some links that can't be made, and that should not, indeed, be attempted. On a local level, someone recently offered me a recording supposedly made of Syd Barrett strumming a guitar behind his fence – a microphone had been strategically placed to catch the erratic chords. This is material that should not be available to me, but a neighbour listening nearby who hears it randomly might justifiably stand and listen. On the other hand, rare studio recordings of Syd Barrett that circulate don't seem to fit the category of personal intrusion. It's a strange analogy, but a workable one – there are poetries that should not be made available to all leaders and listeners, as there are words, rituals, artworks, and pieces of music that belong to particular contexts and places. The process of publication and editing is a political one. This is why I am strongly against the publication of Aboriginal song-cycles that have been collected by white anthropologists. It's simply not the non-indigenous publisher's right to access such materials at will.

So what are we trying to achieve through "internationalising" poetry? On one level, we're talking about enriching respect and intra-cultural understanding, on another about a global linguistic tourism. The latter is obviously an undesirable side product of the former. The internet is recognised as the stimulus for the rapid rise of an international consciousness, and for a consciousness that exists in a non-geo space. A parallel world. A place of community where the boundaries are more flexible and language more fluid. But is this the case in reality? Boundaries and territories exist on the net as much as anywhere else. Prejudices of the real world persist and multiply in cyberspace. You can have small-minded inward looking poets on the net as much as you can in the outside world. People use it to promote their own work as much as to bring attention to others. The desktop becomes the coffee shop. And so on. You have your poets who publish only on the net, and those who see it as a second-rate place to publish. There are "topline" internet journals, and second-rate internet journals. In a field where self-publishing is the norm, there are strong moves towards creating hierarchies. An awareness of place beyond one's own may have been prompted by the net, but in the end it is subject to the conditions of social relations that operate in the outside world.

One of the great uses of the net is in creating these alternative communities (along with their own boundaries and languages, etc.). The invigoration of poetry at the level of language is seen daily on discussion lists and in web collaborative projects. I have co-written two books via email, and numerous pamphlets. It is easy to cut and paste and interact with another writer's words. An active – cybernetic – text emerges. The possibilities are endless. With the poetryetc email discussion list, which I have run over the last few years, a number of projects have emerged and been developed. Poetryetc also runs a Featured Poet series – in fact, we are well into the third series now. Poets as diverse in technique and voice and location as John Tranter (Australia), Michelle Leggott (New Zealand), Alice Notley (USA via Paris), Nils-Ake Hasselmark (island of Arholma), Jo Shapcott (UK), and dozens of others have been run. Each feature carries a statement by the author, a selection of poems, and a biographical note.

One of the most successful projects to be run was the Interactive Geographies Project, which will be published by Salt in book form later this year. It basically functions as a long prose poem. People were invited to write about the space they were "in", in the following way:

> I'd like to invite Poetryetc participants to assist in the creation of a geo-text. The aim is to break down territories, boundaries, demarcation lines etc. by creating an interactive regionalism. If people would send to the list responses to their immediate surroundings – responses to location, demographics, spiritual signifiers, gender, and so on – I'll work the collective effort into a single text and publish it as a Salt book. Your responses should be without punctuation and in continuous text – no line breaks. You will be appropriated, altered and mixed. So, maybe Douglas could begin with "Paris", or maybe it's the Alberta Douglas, or maybe Alison in Melbourne, or someone who lives purely in cyberspace. Deserts, oceans, and the maps of circuit boards all welcome. Interact away!

Pieces came in in their dozens – even hundreds. I cut and spliced and mixed the prose poems into one continuous text. Here's a small extract:

> two ferries 30 k town fishers loggers tiger lilies rhododendrons begonias hemlock painters sculptors an island of palm washed up at Santa Ana and down to the spilt warehouses all in the head the paint factories the furniture showrooms sprawled carpenters gardeners farmers deejays carvers electricians plumbers if you crane your neck you can just about see Kings College chapel through the third floor window though normally I keep the blinds closed to cut down reflections off my X-terminal monitor a colleague described mock-enviously as being the size of Rutland actually the view from the other side is better because you've got the Cam even though the gasometer spoils styles canada geese sea lions seals sand unpublished serious echoes remixing Heraclitus like he must be a mountain in Otago while gray kingfishers hunt California and marshhawks stylize hawkeyes by precise lack of coloration in birds earth-bound where else but in newzealand the only raptors are a falcon and a swampharrier a name which reminds me that the worlds tallest flowering plant the eucalyptus regnans is called Mountain Ash by mainlanders but swamp gum in Tasmania most everything is swamp here it seems and the distinction in naming between here and there reminds me of the marketeers and their wiles as they try to superimpose blocked culverts rotting bridges daft dogs fast cars houses and converted barns where the ploughmen set

soil aside to English nature's doubtful taxonomy I walk despite the numbers also walking where there's a train saying good afternoon it's a lovely day in Kew Gardens

This is international regionalism at work. It speaks for itself. Internationalism becomes more than the mixing together bot of names from diverse parts of the planet, more than hybridising poets with different attitudes to form and language, with different ethical and political views; it becomes a voice in itself. If the author is not dead, the author is variegated and multiplied. Those desiring machines have created a cybernetic voice and a place that is unfindable on any map as we know it. This is the stuff of exploration and holds the attendant risks – it is not always desirable for individual voices to be lost to the community. Colonisations can take place without an awareness of a territory even being crossed. These genre-busting exercises, these internationalist footsteps, can't escape the lessons of history. As they say, for every action there's an equal and opposite reaction. One project's freedom is another's compromise. Not all words and all textual environments are up for grabs. These are not merely verbal games. The globalisation of text must also carry respect for the specific. Individual authors will no doubt recognise their words in the piece quoted above, but the words have become part of the whole, part of the metaphor of the poem itself. All participants agreed that individual contributions would not be identified – indeed, due to the "mixing" process, this is impossible; but the names of all "players" will be included in the front of the publication. A couple of recent postings I sent to the list are as much about a view of "internationalism" as they are about poetryetc:

> The reason this list was set up in the first place was to illustrate that different poetics/pov/geographies/cultures etc (the etc. being the most important part to my mind) can find common ground for dialogue.

and

> Just a note re stats: membership of this list has been fluid from the early listbot days. The number of women on the list at any one time has varied from just under fifty percent to just under thirty-three percent. One of the prime directives of the list is to recognise the truth behind what Mairead and Alison and many others have observed (the archives of poetryetc and poetryetc2 carry some pretty pointed comments by Tracy Ryan, re this)... List membership is open and I actively encourage women to join. You'll note that there's a fair balance re the Featured Poets. I take these points extremely seriously. Thanks for your comments! And poetryetc is a "neutral" (and) safe space – at least that's what it's working towards.

The grounds rules for poetryetc were: no racism, misogyny, or bigotry of any kind. The list has members who are leading poets and critics, people who would normally be seen as being in opposing "camps" (the concept of "camps" has been hotly debated lately) communicate and interact on a regular basis, and people who are just starting to write poetry or are only interested in reading and discussing it all find a home on poetryetc. There are linguistic innovators and formalist poets, there are cross-genre enthusiasts and traditionalists, you name a binary and it's there, and it's surely been broken. And it is international in its membership.

In promoting an internationalism, I feel that one should be wary of ignoring responsibilities in one's own backyard. This is the regionalism issue again. In my case, the degradation of land, the ecological disaster that is modern farming in the Avon Valley, a murderous history of displacement of the Nyungar people, and the obligation to actively support the pursuit of land rights, are just some of the issues that inform whatever I do or say, in whatever context. This is where my so-called "anti-pastoral" comes from. It is easy to make generalisations as an internationalist, to forget the importance of context. There are universal truths, but environment shouldn't be forgotten, despite the claims of certain geneticists!

I once wrote a poem about my Uncle Jack "trusting no more than his own". My family live in York, about seventy miles out of Perth in the Avon Valley. It's wheat and sheep territory. My brother is a shearer, my uncle a farmer. Uncle Jack has never understood why people need to go "elsewhere". He reckons there's enough for a lifetime to do and learn where you're born. He has that rare ability, like my brother, to divine water. I always felt as a child that this gave him a head start – the ability to be in two places at once, to speak another language and know another space.

Poetryetc can be found via its homepage at:
http://www.mailbase.ac.uk/lists/poetryetc/

THE INTERNATIONAL BRIGADE

TWO POEMS BY JOHN KINSELLA
KILLING THE WORLD

"...and the Nationals began to tremble in their boots. The guns, plainly, were costing them but it was not clear how.

The same country bloke gave me a theory. It's the women, he said. They are the ones who watch perturbed while their husbands, rifle in hand, walk up and down the living room raging against the world and drinking some more. They hate guns."
      Bob Ellis, Goodbye Jerusalem

Gun cabinet as magic box,
illusionist's coffin, repository
of the hardest stuff – Alamo,
Eureka stockade, Hitler's bunker,
riot control centre at Pentridge or Alcatraz.
It's the glory chest for the war
against federation, against taxation,
against greenies and ferals,
lesbians, feminists, and homos,
blacks and lefties, vegetarians
and Asians, that bastard
who sold you a dud car
back in '92, a dinner gone cold,
an empty beer fridge,
drought and flood,
sex, sluts, unions,
politicians and the cops.
Beyond technology: gun metal,
guest-host and family,
inhibited chemistries . . . alone
as grog cuts phonelines,
and the buzzing gets louder:
click click inside the box
that insurance companies
and police registrations
can't quite stop. Buy-back
and calibre . . . muzzle velocity,
what fucking right? Stoked-up.
It's so damn loud
and hot in here. Bitch!
Don't look at me like that.

REVERSAL

"In the decade that followed, Aboriginal labour, forced and free, proved a boon at York during the wheat harvest and many crops would have rotted in fields without their help. The use of Aboriginal police constables in the 1840s guaranteed the settlers a trouble-free district. The resistance of the York Nyungars was at an end; their numbers declined, their strength was sapped, their people dispossessed, their vital harmony with their land and the Dreaming irreparably shattered."

Neville Green, Broken Spears: Aboriginals and Europeans in the southwest of Australia

Recollection works as backdrop
and anchors image: the haze,
waves of heat that stretch out
across denuded hills,
gentle folds rock-picked
and cut to the quick, stookers
having a bite to eat under York Gums
by the top gate, car doors wide open
and a waterbag passed around.
A Nyungar family
from the fringe of town.
An articulation
across a fragmenting line,
Needlings stark in the background,
driving slowly past
watching each other vanish,
the city uneasy in the south.
Thirty years back. Reconfigure –
scrub, sound of truck, layout.
It's just a picture, a glimpse
that brought emotions
lost to childhood
in a district of faults
and crevices. Early settlers
garnished kitchens with ears
of murdered Nyungars:
they fear the spirits of their dead.
Knowing the heat
each stalk of wheat
holds in itself: the colour

of florescence. It is language
that contracts. Its growth, illusory.
A sign appears on the rust road:
    Sheep Crossing.
Harvest done, coronas mark fields –
seen and heard by none,
the season turned upside down.

Where It Lives

PHILIP SALOM'S ROUTES TO POETRY

As Mahomet said, talking of location –
Spirit (and I re-phrase, for writers – Language)
lives closer in you than your jugular.

THE FIRST POET of any sort I met was Irish, and the first poet of substance, only a year or so later, was a grim-faced Ted Hughes – fresh, or not so fresh, from his awful encounter with the "Wife Killer!" brigade at Adelaide Writers Week. Hughes read a generous selection of the *Crow* poems and I felt some fundamental cosmic ground shift, balanced just recently by hearing him read on radio the powerful Ovid translations he had recorded shortly before his death. What a marvelous poet he was. The first good poet I spent much time with was William Hart-Smith, born in England, schooled in Scotland and England, initiated into poetry in New Zealand and best known in Australia – as a maker of understated but crisply imagist poems which he began styling before anyone here took the slightest notice of Pound or William Carlos Williams.

By then in his late 60s, Bill Hart-Smith talked about poetry and metaphysics and ancient history most of the time, though he refrained from discussing that other international poetry – fishing – because of my blank lack of interest in that one. Our conversations ranged widely in time and space, therefore; we traveled in talk and imagining like chair-sitting versions of his great hero Christopher Columbus. I felt Bill was very much a man of my own heart. And yet he felt all his life that he was placeless. He envied the Aborigines their sense of country, the rootedness which was not a bind but a spiritual double-arrow of belonging. Crucially, he was the one who studied my poems over several months and pronounced me a poet – and so started me on the journey into the country where I feel I truly belong – the English language. I was converted. Only later did I appreciate how lucky we are, how truly international our language is.

* * * * *

Hart-Smith told me of an odder conversion, which I love: he'd been conducting Adult Education classes in New Zealand in the '30s and was billeted at a farm for a week. He and the farmer's wife would talk poetry every night after dinner while the disgruntled farmer watched them, bored, eventually nodding off in his chair. On Saturday the farmer said he'd show Bill a bit of the real bloody world, took him out onto the farm and gave him a terrible day of hard work. By evening Bill was wrecked. But the farmer was impressed, so he asked this skinny poet what this poetry stuff was. Bill read him his favourite shorter poems by poets he loved, from various countries, and in translation, and some of his own quirky pieces. Months later he rang the farmer's wife. She told him he wouldn't believe it: her husband went out to the shed every morning and while he warmed the kerosene tractor up on petrol, before "turning it over" onto kero, he would take a book of poetry from the bookshelf he'd build and read for ten minutes. Every day. And what poets did this provincial old bugger read? Theodore Roethke and Anna Akhmatova and Robert Frost and Fernando Pessoa.

* * * * *

The deepest voice of my childhood was no poet's but the seismic rumble of Paul Robeson. I am attracted to voices that stand so far out of us they're in us – and Robeson was that to the limit. The ache of the people. I lived on a farm five miles from a small town with one row of shops in the south west of Western Australia. We had only one record of Robeson but then we had very few records of anything: a few 78s of the rather smarmy beauty of Mario Lanza – only his high notes reached where Robeson sang all the time – some ballads by another deep but empire-man Peter Dawson, and some sweet Tchaikovsky and Ponchielli ballet music. I went nowhere but Robeson and much else came through the radio at home, the ABC we listened to day and night. But especially at night. I imagine myself sitting, staring over at the valve radio glowing in the corner, a big wood and Bakelite model, the most special thing in the house, dark and dead until the soft click as you turned it on then light and soul (an almost metaphysical buzz) the inner distances of sound, of voices.

Poetry came much later. Before poetry there was provincialism and the voice. Rural Australia of the '50s was provincial in the extreme: it was daytime and farming; it was, remembering our fathers had just returned from war, shadowed by the slouch hat and the ambushing emotions of heroism and sacrifice; it was The News; and as absolute high point in our little lives – Test cricket. All boys wanted – when we grew up – was to make the team. But during the night hours, from that radio, from the ABC and BBC voices, I absorbed an inner world which paradoxically ranged wider and further by far than the daytime: I absorbed documentaries, dramas, talk shows and comedy.

Like many writers, as a child I read anything. Stacks of Agatha Christie and detective fiction, American cowboy books (amazing now but very prevalent then). I read Rider Haggard and Africa as England saw it. Every week I waited for my adored comics, *Knockout* and *Eagle*. Yes, English comics. Then came Isaac Asimov and Arthur C. Clarke and the worlds out "there". My imagination was offshore or off the planet nearly all the time, except for romances with schoolgirls. Even there I cast myself as the Phantom and her as Diana!

There are only so many places we can carry with us; later, we find them like a stark nostalgia projected throughout the world. I was still collecting them. I was 20 and working on a cattle research station in the wheatbelt when I read *The Vivisector* by Patrick White and was utterly thrown. Powerful, even sardonic, vision from an Australian writer who created an artist's life wrought with demons and ambition. And then *The Aunt's Story* where a woman ends her life in a swirl of Australian-European upheaval and deeply Other realities. Both these novels have Apocalyptic undercurrents. And it hit me head on. I put those books down a changed person. You might say I left the country.

I discovered poetry: T. S. Eliot and his intellectual and European ghosts and voices; Ted Hughes, whose primal earth-energies made immediate sense; then the Americans, starting with Robert Lowell and his musical opposite Wallace Stevens. This was the place for me. Language and memory and the thrill of compressed form. Not nation. Nationalism has never meant much to me. We have seen too much of its obsessions, intensities and – as Heaney has written – its tribal revenge. Poetry is the antidote, the other-music. The "voice" of poetry struck me not as a speaking to or from a nation and not as any mere self-expression but as a way of belonging through metaphor and perception, through engagement with the strategy of line and poem, through meaning and emotion, to the experience of being alive and between nations. It is quietly exhilarating.

Sitting in a corner food-house in Pasir Panjang Road as if the heat wasn't bad enough and the wok-hot air, we have to argue over Conrad's *Heart of Darkness* to know whose heart it was, if Conrad, as Chinua Achebe sternly puts it, sucked up to the English, was a racist. Sikh, Chinese, three others from our different nations, sit equating one degree from the Equator, we straddle the centre of the world.

I have moved repeatedly throughout my life, though never in traumatic circumstances, and usually by decision. This includes living in Italy, Asia and New Zealand as well as other international shorter-term touring. I adapt easily. When young I suppose I was self-centred; and now I'm a poet (heard that one before?). But the shift is important – now there is a purpose to my imaginings, to the introspection and the self-searching. I am restless. Like poetry itself, this is a state of mind, but unlike poetry, restlessness is without form. I find its form in the poems. Sean O'Brien has said of my poems: "Salom seems at home with a permanent state of dislocation". Maybe it's true. Maybe it's also seeing the other poetries, even those other international forms such as science, music, architecture. In Singapore:

> Just now, a faint wind blowing, I note designs:
> four buildings with the violent but static lines
> found only in art and heaven. It is more the slang
> – saying post-modern. One is Leger-like with hanging pipes, tubes, design as disembowelment.
> Only metaphor can say it.

I love the physical things of the world, the fast hungers, food and alcohol and sex, and the long slow rhythms of season, all of which I am alert to and affirm. The other country, however, is the haunting one I cannot forget, and whose voices I am more than curious about, hungry for and, intellectually, even spiritually, restless to hear.

* * * * *

I now feel those early experiences of listening to the radio and wandering alone through the paddocks of a farm, especially in late afternoon in "the hurt-out yellow light of sunset" planted the music and beginnings of poetry, the glimmering apprehensions. The other poetries. Many years later, driving through Italy, I remembered the farm at sunset and that world-voice and knew the heart recognises likeness everywhere:

> Pain is everywhere in earth and stone
> like retribution. Sometimes pain is more
> of air than earth, lifts inside the wind,
> or on the louvres of the light.
> For all the birds in it, it never leaves.
> Put down first by agony, then death,
> then all who lived with it, then by
> the passionate magicians, the Taviani,
> who roll the rich emulsion into film.

My own poetry has been influenced by all the poets I've mentioned and at a later stage quite crucially by Pablo Neruda and Octavio Paz, among others. But I cannot imagine writing without the company of whole bookshelves of poets and, tractor or no tractor, by Anna Akhmatova, by those idiosyncratic *Dream Songs* of John Berryman, or Emily Dickinson's nervy lightning, without the deep music of the Caribbean poets, the humour and irony of Zbigniev Herbert, the almost perilous surrealism of a Tomaz Salamun. I have been fortunate to have won some attention for my own poetry and to have read, by myself and with poets from around the world, in the UK, Canada and the US, Italy, the former Yugoslavia, S. E. Asia and New Zealand. Between nations.

Not everyone has been so free to travel. Pramoedya Ananta Toer, the Indonesian writer who has been nominated for the Nobel several times, spent most of his 70 years incarcerated under the Dutch, then Sukarno, and Suharto (Pram was nothing if not consistent). His words so dangerous they're praised, pored over. His life, therefore, given this grammarian's surveillance: these men all turn him like the dial of a telephone, reporting they hear the voices Marx and Lenin.

In 1998 Pram was allowed for the first time to apply for a passport. Until then his work had traveled for him. He had been invited to America before but this time, unbelievably, he was free to go. Old and chain-smoking, he spoke and read to his many fans in that quite other country, people who greeted him with tumultuous and emotional ovations.

What have **Welsh bards** to do with **gardens**?

Find out in the new *Historic Gardens Review*

"A fresh perspective on garden heritage"

For details and a **free back copy** contact:
Historic Gardens Review, 34 River Court, Upper Ground, London SE1 9PE.
Tel: 020 7633 9165 Fax: 020 7401 7072
e-mail: histgard@aol.com
Website: http://members.aol.com/histgard/

TWO POEMS BY JANE YEH
LOVE IN A COLD CLIMATE

On the ring road heading south, south of Manchester
Past the crumbling mountains' edges, irregular against the sky, you

Steer, clearing the thin & swooning back-roads, swervers
Through all the hills of these states, where the spindly trees' trunks rise in masses

From out the cut-granite ground, their leaves
Half alive. There is no landscape where we were driving

In the crumpled corner of the north – only high sides of rock,
A facing of trees, & the small spaces threading between. In

The convoluted heart of this other England, we were stunning
The way an anomaly of weather patterns snarled over water is stunning,

But lasting no longer than an instant – & this autumn, out on
The motorway you follow the local forecast

Through Worcester & Cambridge, down into Greenwich, on the air-
Waves' heavenly progress to your car.

PARIS, 1899

Where the trees are thick in their trunks, hard-veined
& pronounced of silhouette. They are disdainers

Knowing how everything fits together, poised among their own
Old world. *I was made for destruction, too improbable*

For this century. When the gas-lights go on they crush together
Awkward & flaring, unschooled in flattery. *They mock me.*

If the day comes I shall stand before you: uncertain
Of voice, unsteady of feature. I shall barely remember

How to signal assent with my hands, much less the words
Orchidaceous & belated, least of all

How I am to account for the distance
Between the shimmering, fantastical concoction of my past

& the thing I have become. *How can you find me
Utterly your own one, still?* Along the fraying edges of hems

Our misalliance wanders like pick-stitch, quite crooked
& vanishing when reversed. *We shall not meet again.*

When the day comes I am sure to feel nothing
Even as the continent is slowly shifting, & over

The waters of bells of Trinity & Magdalen are faint in their calls, faintly
Swinging, & when that day comes past the houses

In Tite Street the hyacinths will be languid
& astonishing in their finery. *Turn, counterturn, stand.*

ISTVÁN VÖRÖS
THE DAY OF WATER

At the bottom of bad decisions,
like rain-water, there's always the sediment
of some good. It's worth fishing out the leaves
drifting in it, and moving the barrel from
beneath the eaves. If you enter the
house where you haven't been all winter,
mind your step. You find on the carpet
the dry bodies of bugs that have
wintered there, and when you begin to sweep them,
two thirds make it onto the dust-pan,
but the third flies up, beating
with faded wings on the window.
Let them go free, or use
the bug-spray, no one will judge you, and
even if you feel regret, acquiescence is
seeping through the walls of your decision.
First only slightly, but then as if you were
standing at the bottom of an emptied well,
saying you did the right thing, no place
for bugs in the house, and up

sprouts the water, it reaches your ankle, or
rather, let them live, once they've survived
winter, now it reaches the top of your
rubber boots and the cold flow gushes
into them: I, you hear the water
speak out, and then not I, it says.
When it floods you above the belt
you call out for the ladder to be
handed down, you made the right choice, comes
the answer, or the wrong one, but never
you mind. The level of water is now up to
your throat. There were fish, too, in the water,
someone calls down again, and this is the last
thing you hear, for already you see them
gaping, one of them signals for
you to follow, how much longer can
this take, you go obediently,
your gills, not having been used
for so long now, keep stalling.
In the underwater throne chamber
you are led to the king, you made
the right choice, letting them go free,
he says, then you are led to the hang-
man, you made the wrong choice,
killing them, he says,
and has a hook with cake-
bait float before you, and then
the water begins to ebb
the well parts, as though from a bubble
on the surface, and you fall, coughing,
spitting water, fainting on
the grass. In winter you pace
in an empty house, not I,
the water gurgles in the drains.
At the bottom of good decisions – a few
dry leaves, a fist-sized
snail – there is always
some sediment.

Translated by Zsolt Komáromy

TWO POEMS BY TOM FRENCH
'NATIONALISM IN MUSIC' (1982)

The only surviving recording of your voice
is the school music project on a tape cassette
they shipped home with your personal effects.
My ghost cognoscente, my musical enthusiast,
I wanted to ask what difference music makes,
rewinding it for months to hear you pronounce
"Na-a-a-a-tionalism" and *"nineteen-tirty-tree"*,
the great names *"Borodin, Smetana, Mussorgsky"*.
I think I should have seen you in your cask,
touched your broken legs, your smashed wrists,
rested my palms against the bruise of your face.
When I play it now I play it to hear, more
than anything else, *"the music that springs
directly from the earth, from no apparent source"*.

BLOOD

She returns the Visa you gave her in error,
takes your hand and pricks your little finger.
By the time the drop of your blood she releases
hits rock bottom you know her from somewhere,
so you take the plunge and ask her to supper
to a cybercaf on the outskirts where the waitress
palms what you slip her for a booth in the corner.
When the cashier swipes it, the machine accepts
your blood donor card, though you're in the red,
and a couple of bottles of the house plonk later
her uniform is draped on the back of a chair
and she's kissed the vein in your forearm better.
The tiny silver Pelican that comes weeks later
draws a dark red pearl from the identical finger.

TWO POEMS BY ADAM SCHWARTZMAN
THE LAST THING

When I drove and I drove and I drove to Knysna   and the shacks were falling down the hills
to the sea   and the road opened like light

adhering to the edges of a brass bell
and the dark hills lined up   like wise men

and the distances tore past under my feet   and then I could not bear
                                                            its tearing any more
and the crickets rattled in my ears

the last thing I felt was your touch
like pale blind fish in a cave   but that will pass.

When my ribs opened   like two red fans
and my breath   came out like rivers, and caught on the stones
         and spilled

and all I heard   was the stars marrying with the pale grass
(it was the sound of a hundred falling   silver leaves)

 the last thing I saw was your face, blind as the moon   but that will pass.

When the sky folded away   my affairs,
and I slipped from my skin   as from a shining wrapper
and I lay above myself like smoke above a veld   as well as like muddy water
and I no longer had a body
the last thing I knew   was your body
like a snake wrapped in its tissue skin   but that will pass.

And when the bushes and stones pecked at me
and I thinned   like honey-comb

and you whispered to me
again and again
the last thing I heard   was the ants crawling in my head

and when I was gathered up in blanket of sand
and the grass and the trees drew me up
and the stone of me   opened up like a bean

and I pushed into the air   as if tying many knots through it
and then I was in the air

the first thing I tried to weave round
was you

but that will pass.

SACRED FOREST

A little way   on the forest was bringing itself down tree by tree
the bark was unpeeling itself   cracking in the air
and the spirits were pouring out of the roots   and the birds were rustling and clicking.

The stone gods grew from the roots,   flat stone women
whose fingers exploded like bananas
and their breasts were like pointed desert fruit.
Around them the vines of the forest coiled   hissing like electricity cables.

Suddenly a river came round the bend,   pulling pieces of light down its way;
the monkeys began praying to the river.
We were in the widest, coolest place, where the skies were growing
and falling away,   the forest was moving.
I put my forehead on the foot of the god and the cool forest jumped into me,
and the birds turned madly like rusted gates.

Further on the river came to cut us off   but the banks spring a bridge
and the hair of the river twisted away around the rocks.
You be no man   came the forest in me,
You now be no man,
and the river flipped a curl up the bank and tapped my ankle
Now you be no man-o!

TWO POEMS BY MONICA YOUN
AFTER FRANZ KLINE

In what box is it buried – that first
fossilized dawn? What thing in me survived

the sight of you nosing through the bedsheets
for each shed strand of my black hair, before

ten-years-my-elder Allison got home?

ALASKA VARIATIONS

The blue latex of the glacier's glove
on the mountain's furred shoulder,

scrabbled stones on the river path,
a bell to ward off bears. 5 p.m.

The dark drifts down in a fine powder:
fulminate of mercury. October's rust-red

moulting salmon seem motionless,
but we know the gray river is moving,

as we know it makes its own noise
under the bear bell's bright

lifesaving chime. Blue "from compression",
so I'm told, but why compression

should be blue I couldn't
tell you. Salmon like axe-heads

in the gray back of a beast. Gunpowder
trickles from the mountain's loose fist.

The bear bell hangs a bridle of bottles
over the gravid river. Blue Gore-tex

windbreaker, bell strapped to wrist: "Keep moving.
Try to sound as human as you can".

TWO POEMS BY SARAH WARDLE
SCEPTIC'S SONG
After Montale

I fear one day, as I walk down the street,
I shall see through the window of the world.
Looking over my shoulder, my eyes will meet
a void, no drunk's vision, but a vacant whirl.

Then reality will vanish, the reel turn
and illusion again be projected on
all nothingness, but in me the truth will burn,
for I'll know that I too am part of the con.

TO THE READER

The words I write become another world,
where I am both the poem and the maker,
the creator, who decides what light is called,
and the *logos*, which is uttered by the speaker,
and in this place virtual love is possible,
and for the best in a parallel universe,
and happens on a planet the size of a pebble,
when you and I invisibly move the earth,
but this poem is only one of many
amid all the pages lost on library shelves,
and that planet revolves round an infinity
of other worlds and other people's selves,
and my pebble lies with millions on the beach,
where you might choose it, then skim it out to sea.

TWO POEMS BY BRIAN HENRY
DISCRETE MATHEMATICS

Though the odds were against me
I opted for the catastrophic policy
and immediately booked a seat in coach
to a country where the language is easy
to ignore, the food cheap and diseased,
and the women, the women are like the food.
It felt like heaven, or the closest
a former photocopier repairman will ever get
to a toner-free demesne. No doubt
the powerful are at fault for everything ugly.
My shoes, for example, provide comfort
but are lacking in the style brigade –
clearly the work of a steroid
-ridden cobbler. My ex-girlfriend,
a knockout at fourteen
in her size 1 Guess jeans, has become,
in the short twelve years since we broke up,
mother material. I am not the father side
of her equation. I prefer inequalities,
especially when they gesture
toward the potential for *equal to*.
Don't get me started on anti-
derivatives.
               When bored, which is often,
I create my own numerical systems
and make up laws specific to each variable.
My current system, Lois, enjoys
buffets, parlor tricks, and pantoums.
She is a discernible improvement
over my previous system, Lester,
who, alas, had a penchant for ill-groomed hares
regardless of political affiliation.
Nine times out of seventy-two a cancer cell
will wreck the house it burgles.
That sounds officially interesting
but no one knows about the remaining sixty-three.
I like to think that's where the police come in.
The burden of proof knows no borders
except when smashed into a four-by-four matrix.

I spent the first twelve months of my pregnancy
composing a linear sequence.
                          In the end it curved.

LIPOSUCTION

In a trance of fat, with a fattened stance
the man expands
to points beyond expectation *and* reason,
his hand-to-mouth on the move and in season –
the months of non-stop consumption
that yearly yields scores of pounds eager for redemption
at the surgeon's, where cells
are drawn like dustballs
into a vacuum pump's pump,
the hose playing hooker to fat's pimp
as the man swells in and out
of consciousness, gnawing his hand in its shackle,
a bit of skin stuck, bloodless, to his mouth,
the surgeon's assistant hissing "What a fuckknuckle".

The surgeon's assistant hissing "What a fuckknuckle",
the man awakes, hand-in-mouth,
shakes his wrist in its shackle
until the assistant turns up the gas and he's out. . .

The man awakes, hand-in-mouth,
having dreamt of a girl, a pimp,
until the assistant turns up the gas ("– and he's out!"),
the surgeon still manning the pump.

Having dreamt of a girl, a pimp,
the ones who had him by the wallet, the balls,
the surgeon, still manning the pump,
is rattled, misses a few cells.

The ones who had him by the wallet, the balls,
launched the surgeon on the road to redemption,
his rattled missus, a few fat cells
less a consideration than *in medias consumption*.

Launched, the surgeon on the road to Redemption
IN, hopes to make it to camp before the start of the season;
less a consideration than immediate consumption,
his dream his only reason.

In hope of making it to camp before the start of the season,
the surgeon focuses, expands
– his dream his only reason –
eyes his assistant, misunderstands

the hissing ("What a fuckknuckle"),
assumes it's meant for the man in his trance,
who shakes his wrist in its shackle.

Catching the Drift

by Andrew Osborn

MARK LEVINE
Enola Gay
University of California Press, £8.95
ISBN 0 520 22260 1

LIKE *AS YOU* Like It, Mark Levine's long-awaited second book concludes with a quadruple marriage, but his wedding party is less tractable than Shakespeare's cross-dressers, less cogent than country fools, and the color of comedy has been cloroxed. Groom one comes off as an ambitious Molotov cocktail: "All the impatient green bottles were pairing off, / a few stuffed with dainty Spanish galleons. / I doused my rag in silvery boutane. / I had a picnic to attack: lamb chops; childhood". Groom two gets wooed by a breeze "to slumber in its [yes, the breeze's] physicist's truck". In part three, "my only lonely bride" is found "squatting in shadows beneath the fuse box, / distracted by trumpets". Pretty bleak. I don't mean to suggest that the felicitous social integrations crucial to the comic are likewise essential to lyric – far from it. Just know that the unpromising matches in 'Wedding Day' reflect the uneasy relationships many of Levine's new poems seem to seek from their readers.

Enola Gay begins at the altar, as well. In 'Then for the Seventh Night', the speaker finds himself ("again") in a dilapidated church, mouthing the unfamiliar words of a song his mother's "long absence implied, though his voice / was not good and even he distrusted his voice". That Levine's voice is good – or was good, and promised to "stay good for days" – anyone could have heard in *Debt*, Jorie Graham's 1992 pick for the National Poetry Series. Interlacing a confusion of the theatre of dramatic performance and the theater of war with quotations from Matthew Arnold, 'About Face (A Poem Called "Dover Beach")' implied that to be a belated poet means always to hear one's own voice, one's own lines, from "Behind enemy lines? Yes. Toujours". And no persona endured intact through any given poem, let alone the collection ("I am a zipper. A paper cut. / I fed myself so many times / through the shredder I am confetti, / I am a ticker-tape parade, I am an astronaut / waving from my convertible at Henri"). Instead, it was this drive to redefine the self that remained in force, manifest as a voice of near-rabid intensity speaking through the mouth-holes of multiple, tear-away masks. *Debt* showed us what happens to identitarian poetics when the poet is a paradoxical hybrid of cultural types ("Both 'A' and 'Not-A'"). When the fence-picket he's been sitting on goes on strike, he takes up a bullhorn.

Enola Gay wields no "calm Jew terror", no Wild West Quixote, and no resourcefully protean Henri. The voice of *Debt* echoes most clearly through

'Eclipse, Eclipse' ("A pencil in his glove and a shovel in his soul / and big plans for a secret farm: comes a horseman") and 'Unlike Graham', whose eponym is ostensibly a fellow male patient in a psychiatric ward (though how can we not imagine a wink at Jorie?). I hear it, too, though the sentences are longer, the phrasing less clipped, in the first three-and-a-half lines of 'Susan Fowler' ("The question seemed fair game to him, though the wind / was blowing strongly and the bearded man was speaking / too rapidly and the precise content of the question / could not be made out") and the last three of 'The Response' ("Each time I try to speak he finishes / my sentences for me in unexpected ways. / And he is right").

The catchiest poems in *Enola Gay* share and even notch-up, make more rhythmic, *Debt*'s manic momentum. 'Jack and Jill' is about a person – yes, one paradoxical hybrid – by that name: "He was hungry. Was he real? / Was he a rhyme? Was he a trace / of purple smoke escaped from base? / He'd taken a great spill – // he swallowed rain; he had a taste / of precious metals and malaise". In this poem and others like the highly gratuitous but fun '*How Pleasant to Know Mr. Lear* by Edward Lear', run-amok rhyming bespeaks a what-the-hell attitude: since nothing in this world is fundamental, one might as well let the accidents of sound dictate where one goes. Similarly memorable and quaint are those prosy anecdotes for which Levine's new-found interest in metricality and rhyme's odd couplings make way. 'My Friend' recounts a cat-call-gone-heart-to-heart reminiscent of James Tate's sad clowning. 'Everybody' drifts lazy-lovey through "the happiest moment / Of everybody's life"; imagine O'Hara writing a lunch poem while tubing down the Monongahela.

By far my favorite new poem, one of the most intriguing I've read this year, 'Winter Occasional' combines *Enola Gay*'s measured patience and willingness to let sound steer with a nod to *Debt*'s imaginative clarity. The goings-on in that first book were so succinctly described that, even at their most surreal, one never questioned what one was asked to see. Tolouse is a piece of cardboard? Fine. The mayor paints it blue so you can fish in it? Fine. This remains important because Levine's personae do, regularly, question such things ("One eye disavowed what the other eye saw"). A grammatical negative of his earlier "I"-intensive litanies, 'Winter Occasional' omits the personal subject altogether: "Stayed too long. Was made to see the thing. / Made to handle it, to scrape it clean". I think of Acteon's accidental, chronic sighting of Diana. But it is the vagueness of "the thing" encountered and the precision with which it must be known that motivates the poem and its readers to grope forward. More varied and suggestive than *Enola Gay*'s several list poems ('The Holy Pail', for example, is a sacred and profane loteria arranged in strong-stress tetrameter), a series of noun phrases do exactly that – grope:

> The strain of heat. The wounded green
> fabric, the thinking, the wan starling
>
> crumpling into a stray eastbound train
> in a flooded forest: Poland. Ice
> in paper cups with sparkling juice.
> Supper for two and two blue flames.

And when, like a small berg of frozen feeling, "like a many- / edged memory of the heroic clan: / the snow-queen descends", she rides on her own melting, as Frost said good poems should. The abba rhymes of the first four quatrains are sure-edged and stark enough that a certain slant in the fifth and last accentuates its note of menace:

> Mistook her hole for mine. Was bled.
> Was made to pierce her tent with light.
> The air was tilted at an awkward angle
> And tasted, like lead, of the other side.

Dickinson (see especially #341), removed from cryogenesis at last.

Elsewhere, however, *Debt*'s martial hazards and bureaucratic hazing have given way to an oneiric haziness. Whatever associations bind the title poem and many others including each of the five poems titled 'Lyric' elude me. While Levine's props have become more organic, his cognitive sequencing has become less so. Empty, ugly lines – like "Take me to your place in your place, will you not?" – crop up. These days, lyric's cutting edge probes the borders of understanding and empathy, which is fine, even fascinating; Levine probes well into the other side, however, and the results sometimes taste leaden. I assume he is aiming for what Stevens called the pleasures of merely circulating; the second 'Lyric' begins, "At the very least. / Lines circulated. People and their braces, speech-flakes, dogged music". I, for one, want more from Levine than Ashberian speech-flakes. At the risk of running into that snow-queen, I want to catch his drift.

Some will say that such lyric disintegration is symptomatic of, and appropriate to, a life made imaginable by real-world events like the dropping of Little Boy on Hiroshima. Sure enough, *Enola Gay*'s is a world whose gods, too, must sleep in a cold tent ("They knelt on the gravel / pondering the sky from which they long ago fell"). Still, shouldn't one sing as well as one can and let the cracking of voice take care of itself? If Levine's still singing from his heart and not playing the *eiron*, what does it mean of the last eight years?

TWO POEMS BY MARY JO BANG
ETCHED, TETCHED, TOUCHED

It was perhaps Hollandish. A tinted print
of a functional waterway tearing a town apart.
Aproned ladies and laddies in breeches.
A dog baited by a strip of bacon. Louise didn't care
for such scenes. Static antics, she said. Sterile takes
on quotidian twilight.
Give me rapture and bliss, she told Ham.
Hieronymus Bosch and Mister S. Dali
(her sister Lydia claimed to have seen the latter
her second summer in Montmartre).
The epiphany of Yves Tanguy walking a panther
seaside in Cannes.
Such sights call up the shades, Louise said.
Only they know how to last.
Meaning, forever.
All else shifts the way the print has now tilted
with no one near.
Ham crossed the carpet to right it.
Of course, Louise too could be a pretty picture: a woman
riveted to earth in raiments
right for the season – hilarity on her face,
the boat balanced behind her. From another angle –
a perilous island
of plenty volcanic, tigers hidden in tree tops,
leopards masking the faces
of mountains – an irresistible silence on the edge
of a ruin, warm at the wrist.

TO SAVOR THE SEQUEL

Both happy and simple sad, the hesitant gamut
of where the lovetrain could run – there and back, there
and back, followed by the predictable

fade-out and that might be savored as well, but not likely.
She compared it to dropping
through an infinitude of slow lacerations.
Love, love, love, love, love, love, love—
a hive hum ongoing in the hear ear.
How could that be a thing of pure pleasure?
A fast-footed dance down the hall
that gave onto a vast view of hell. A bell at the door,
a beloved's name just above it.
Come in, come in. And she did as always enter
and she wished as always after
that the sequel might be seen (might be felt) as a form
of recreation, a game tied by two match-match opponents
instead of a chair and a window,
a wisp of ice running through her. The on-going on-going,
she opened the window wider, picked up her pen.
Dear X. Dearest X. What was there to say?
She rose and would no longer write.
The impulse had leaped over an edge,
an undulate verge, ever near, into which would sometimes fall
a tear or two, and however many feelings.

TWO POEMS BY TRACY RYAN
HOMECOMING

As if the hothouse contents had
got loose and gone reeling,
as if a cast were
peeled off & the limb long since
had forgotten the discipline of muscle.
A profusion of blue, the sky, the plumbago
unruly as I remember it, & the blooms
a riot on bougainvillea.
As if my insides had unravelled
& willed themselves
to words: the ancients thought
our gut the seat of emotion. Heart
too clean & purposeful
an emblem for this sprawl, this
letting it all find space. A release,
a return to the wilderness.

LANDING
When I enter you it is always
with the feeling of having forgotten something;
a taint of betrayal not even the
disinfectant spray can disguise, a sense
not that the years or the foreignness
could be stripped away, but that
there really is nothing underneath,
that the offending matter
(wood, straw, fur, seeds, alien soil
ingrained in my skin) moves with me,
with us, the blood
on certain hands, and that your notion
of being some kind of virgin, O most continent
of continents, should have been
lifted long ago from your shoulders, and
though I know these precautions are necessary and
would never willingly transgress, I understand
them too as metaphor: if we're any lady at all, then,
Lady Macbeth.

NOTE: it may be necessary for readers to know that Australia requires planes to be sprayed inside as you land – bizarre experience – and that almost nothing is allowed to be brought in because of diseases of soil & animals etc. I don't know if being sprayed with disinfectant is a common travel tale – it's never happened to me anywhere else.

TWO POEM BY MALINDA MARKHAM

THE PERCEPTIBLE WORLD

All the dishes are blue, and lovely as eyes,

eggs shiny and orange in a dish.
Your hands could be wood and are lovelier for this.
Tonight, fill the spaces with anything at all,
dark strips of seaweed, rice

white as air in the story

where everything separates in pairs, narrow as twigs.
Decorations dusted with flour or salt:
This distance pulls at the breath.

Without touching, how can I know the guests exist?
My own body solemn in its chair,

straight as that candle, its own guttered sun.
No flowers on the table,
the center empty as the curve of an arm.

Fish opened to ribs, petalled gray flesh.
The question has vanished, but I remember your eyes,
all pupil at a distance, walnut up close.

I forget all spelling in the roundness of bowls
and how to pry such memories apart.

FIRST RECEIVED

The wind is sweet here with nothing I can name. Crushed leaves
beside the gate smell thick and dark as letters
between us, bitter to taste. This is a month of watching lotus
court the comparative warmth of the ground. I hear your voice
in strange places, as bats swim around branches,
and water draws night toward its sheen. The statue in the garden
shapes an indifferent gaze. The leaves around her
breathe citrus and the dusk of skin. I think of you
when the last light glints on the rooftiles. I see their order

as one you would admire; from this distance,
delicate and strong as veins in grass. The pond offers nothing
it hasn't received, reflecting the gate and this path. A god,
it swings between tantalus and grief, its surface
skin so soft a hand could push through it. Nothing but algae beneath,
an occasional twig. If the leaves didn't flare and darken on cue,
I would think you'd forgotten. Moss collects
on the usual side of trees. In daytime, girls swing, bright birds,
and scrape their shoes on the ground. They do not fear
falling through it, being light and having no thought of wings.

CLAUDIA RANKINE
LANDSCAPE ABSTRACTIONS TAKEN TO NARRATIVE IN SERVICE OF PLOT

VIEW OF LANDSCAPE I

The cloud in passage as a glimpse of motion read upright,
in constant paraphrase, loosely and in defense of time,
in time laughing at form absorbed, swiftly caught, was
humming in cool ceramic blues, sheep, wool, cotton, rabbit,
fur, flour, fuzz, foam –

The tree, having lived these hundreds of years, caught behind two figures in
speech of speech (language people) lost in the particulars shading the
cultural value of beauty, was feeling respectably stale compared to the steel
girders, a revolving crane.
A road in paralyzed density and grayer where the sun shifts, dumbly insisting
on its completed sacrifice to the long line arriving it at departure,
bringing everything it means, unmistakably personal, to each metaphor
entered.

I am beginning to lose myself, the road insists.
Wipe your face, the tree suggests.
The lines on my face are not of the asphalt originally, the road explains.
Below it perhaps, or beyond.
I see you no matter who, says the cloud.
Pearlesent dusk: white shadows across sky, each tree a point bloomed. And to
speak of loss is like dusting a thought much further away. Further than the
moment when the atmosphere cries, I am lost though I am here.

VIEW OF LANDSCAPE II

A river urged toward its craving, mouthfuls of cerulean and coppery earth
making splashes, its babbling general not naming so not owning, its every
gesture pacific, all its
porcelain refusal crashing over rocks, every amen solved.
A bridge and below the suggested depths absorbed within the busyness of flow.
A splash dissolved, pulled down to glance itself.
The white-bellied bird reflected, intoxicated by the driven
drama, incorporating details in her beak, meaning to build that nest, the
pulsing idea already uttered, digested by this world, expected.
In silvery strokes live the suspension facing horizon, giving
back all that stands: the broadened set reaching out – sun so unraveled, the
day might call it night; the night, dawn lapping luminous, crashing intent to
overdo the gaps fetching forward.

VIEW OF LANDSCAPE III

Rain, unable to break free of narrative constraints, lingers in
the chill lining solitude, giving expression to each breath surrendering.
The waves, caught below, a dying out.
A Virgin plane, hidden turbulence of wind, filled in by dozing.
A captain, turning the seatbelt sign on and off, apologizing for one
particular piece of sky. A stewardess dreaming against an unoccupied stall.
Ice in rain (in the rhetoric of metaphor), a waxen face, graven image,
echoing the romance in the lyric, a solid breath, mist-filled, pure utterance
asserting self, ceding to the whitened gasp blending in as air in ocean, a
life sliced horizontally between living and diving, a state of mind tuned to
its haunting.
To hold cold in the mouth. To speak its shiver. Each shiver the compression
of fear in the terror in losing the self to the self of another name. How is
the rain not "I"? How is the ocean not "I".
Am I only as the surface seems?
Time I know is fluid but in all ways I am drawn into a feeling of solidity.
All that I feel, says the ice, seems all that I will ever be.
The sun is waking, moans the rain. I can't stay.
Of course, says the ice.
Each time, thinks the ice.
Each time and all of us so loosely based.

Goofy Magic

by Sharon Mesmer

TOM DEVANEY
The American Pragmatist Fell In Love
Banshee Press, $10
ISBN 1 9288 2301 7

KIM LYONS
Abracadabra
Granary Books, $12
1 887123 31 8

EDWIN TORRES
Fractured Humorous
Subpress, $10
ISBN 0 9666 3036 X

FOUNDED IN 1966 by the late American poet and translator Paul Blackburn, the Poetry Project, located at St. Mark's Church in Manhattan's East Village, has provided a locus for poets of many backgrounds and literary orientations. The names of those who have performed there comprise a Who's Who of late 20th century American literary tradition: Allen Ginsberg, Adrienne Rich, Patti Smith, Amiri Baraka (LeRoi Jones), Anne Waldman, and Kenneth Koch among many others. Prose writers have always been welcome as well: Alice Walker, William S. Burroughs, and Sam Shepard have performed there. As it makes its way into the 21st century, the Project continues to be a viable and friendly forum for literary talent. The three poets presented here are really just a tiny sampling of the vast range of writers who are associated with the Project by giving and going to readings. (Two of the poets, Kimberley Lyons had Edwin Torres, have worked at the Project: Lyons as assistant director, and Torres as a reading series coordinator.)

It would be impossible to define any overall idea that connects the work of the poets associated with the Project, but there is a feeling of being "in the moment" of the poem that may link the various works thematically, a kind of vibrant immediacy that pervades the language. In his first collection, *The American Pragmatist Fell in Love*, Tom Devaney creates an "as it happens" narration of a lively consciousness wending its way through museums, American advertising, the death of Allen Ginsberg, and the ecstasy of signification in general. The moment is of utmost importance:

> Standing between two rooms at the Museum of
> Modern Art
> one of Jackson Pollocks the other colorfields
>
> I notice in the Pollock room people dispersing in all
> directions
> couples departing, groups ungrouping
>
> people being pulled apart (my wet fall thought)
> down a leafy gutter run-off, where I'm half in, half
> not.

To address the Now is to address the Future; to retain the verity of a moment by presenting it just as it is to create a more vibrant line. As in Roland Barthes' essays on contemporary phenomena (wrestling; plastic; Audrey Hepburn's face vs. Greta Garbo's), the immedate moment is the key to grasping the overarching goofy magic of humanity. In 'The Heartbeat of America Makes Its Own Gravy' the sickeningly familiar riffs of American advertising are organized as a hybrid of the list poem and the litany:

> Nobody doesn't like The crazy new wave in Swiss
> watches.
> Nobody doesn't like Kills bugs dead.
> Nobody doesn't like Tastes so good cats ask for it by
> name.
> Nobody doesn't like It even wipes out pimples you
> don't have.

As a student of previous Poetry Project generations, Devaney references those generations in 'Heartbeat': the poems of the late Joe Brainerd (in particular the famous 'I Remember' list poems, wherein each line begins with "I Remember") and the late Ted Berrigan, perhaps the most conspicuous practitioner of referencing, of the list and the 'Things To Do' structures (in particular 'From A List of Delusions of the Insane: What They Are Afraid Of' and 'Things To Do In Providence', 'Things To Do On Speed'). The litany-like quality of 'Heartbeat' references Allen Ginsberg's Howl.

During his life the most prominent member of the Poetry Project community, Ginsberg was Devaney's teacher, and his death provides the occasion for 'Secret Scribbled Notebook':

> Allen said, "What are you saying?" I said I was trying
> "to be 'ambiguous'".
> "Fuck you and your ambiguity", he said.
> Our meeting was being taped for *Der Spiegel*.

At the end of the poem, he references Frank O'Hara's 'The Day Lady Died' in describing an encounter with another poet on the subway:

> The 2 train's crowded, sit snug talk of Allen's
> ailments . . .
>
> – I'm sweating too by now
> thinking not thinking, a hundred blocks before we
> speak again.

Devaney demonstrates the occasion or "moment" of the poem, a moment which can include even the most mundane of experiences. And always with the overlayment of powerfully personal language and perception, as Devaney himself demonstrates in 'this blues is bullshit':

> smell the stink of nothing stinking
> the overhead lighting won't stick to anything...
>
> a man told me there's a cure for what i have in the fly
> kingdom
> how many other things have i been unable to hear?

In Kimberley Lyons' seventh collection *Abracadabra*, the familiar objects of the human quotidian – appliance cords, sweaters, biscotti, orange formica chairs – are revisioned from and refracted off a certain slant of poetic sensibility that is never really "local" despite its aura of proximity. In reimagining the familiar, Lyons works a rich personal aesthetic: the urbane off-hand referencings of the first generation New York School (who were themselves working from the French surrealist model) and the precise logo-centricism of L=A=N=G=U=A=G=E poetics, are recapitulated in her suave melancholy that in one moment mourns and celebrates the "intangibility of disturbances on the street". And those disturbances – those Rimbaudian "seasons" contained in moments – are the true revelators (and words themselves the agents of revelation). Like a mystic, Lyons believes it's the ordinary everyday stuff that divulges. In 'Details and Incidents', it's

> ... cords of appliances that thwart
> casual obfuscation of objects

that constitute the treasures of the re-visioned landscape. Those ordinary cords, then, are at this very moment refashioning the mundane into the luminous – did you see it? No? Well, there are unlimited opportunities for manifestation. In 'Cafe Silverio', things become other things as a way of demonstrating the equilibrium of outer and inner:

> the ground
> could be the
> roof
> of an inordinate mouth
>
> Stems tweaked
> antennas provoked
> the static interrupts static.
>
> The expository cadence
> of seasons
> melds to other graphic musics.
>
> I felt vertiginous as I looked
> forward into the tunnel of trees ...

Vertiginous indeed. The view is breathtaking, and it changes all the time. Now you're looking at a pile of papers; now a tambourine; now a sweater of "classically obdurate particles". Lyons is a poet of conditions, of moments, the changes, the transformations, the little invisible victories and defeats in the arrivals and departures of thoughts:

> ... patches, duration.
> Rather than continuity,
> spheres, cycles.
>
> I try to write it at a slant.
> Now, not even located.

And what remains, after all, is the magic of pure vision itself:

> a sight unseen requires nothing
> but you gave everything to its beauty

Edwin Torres, more so than Devaney and Lyons, comes out of the performative arena, the "spoken word" movement that reached a kind of apotheosis in the poetry slams (invented, incidentally, in Chicago not New York) held at the Nuyorican Poets Cafe; his work spans the dynamics of both the Nuyorican and the Poetry Project. In Torres' third collection *Fractured Humorous*, issues similar to those found in the works of Devaney and Lyons are addressed – occasion/ moment, pure perception and language as agent of revelation – but are organized around the idea of a fracture (Torres' broken arm) that heals, that brings power to the wound, to the word. The poem 'Roaming as the Roamers Do' acts as a prologue:

> as a hand passed over
> a healing pass – over this
> would be
> this page – containing
> the bits
> that have broken off
> – my pen – my self
> and landed
> on this heal – existing in my fracture

Much attention is paid to organization, spacing, focus, framing, here. Often the poems spill out over the page in different sizes and fonts, or are buttressed with diagrams, arrows, boxed quotes, as if to point out the primacy of the Word, the word-as-agent of revelation (as in Lyons' work). In the book's first section, 'Fracture' which records the history of the poet's broken arm, Torres uses the iconic dictions of American money and media-speak (like Devaney does) combined with "break" puns to convey a mood of goofy illumination. In 'The Eluctionist Is A Boll Weevil Comparing X Rays on Channel 38' the following two lines are boxed, as they might be in a financial prospectus or self-help tome:

> In Seclusion: Allow yourself the remote inversion
> obtained through repetition.
> Only in syndication will the break yield the highest
> quarterly inturns.

Torres also applies the mundane musics of other writings (business, financial, medical scientific) to point out the viability of the non-poetic moment in poetry. From the same poem:

> C. The current climate within the rod is primed for immobility as long as you can stand it There will be swelling followed by periods of DOUBT this is no filmic callous achievement however At 30-second
> intervals
> you WILL be able to charge
> an ABSURDLY HIGH RATE
> merely because this IS the Ratings Sweep that has
>
> ENTERED
> the FRACTURE

Because of Torres' grounding in the spoken word movement, language plays abound, for example in 'Torresian Revelation: 3-16', perhaps the defining moment of the book:

> When I didn't know I was the man – I WAS
> the man. When I wanted to BE
> the man – I was past the point of BEING
> the man... that privilege had been
> passed on – to the new man.
> What I now know as being – was not knowing...
>
> was the BE the BE-er
> or the be – THAT
> be the man!

One gets the impression from reading all three poets that the beauty of the moment is that most times it's so easy to miss. But the important thing is the awareness of the immediate, to be always in the moment, to be as Jack Kerouac said, "submissive to everything, open, listening".

Forthcoming Issues

Autumn: *Reader Power*

The growth of reading groups and the creation of bestsellers by word-of-mouth recommendation has been a feature of general publishing in the last few years. Now the poetry reader gets a look in, with reviews of Adcock, Borges, Causley, Hart Crane, Anne Michaels, Plath &c by reading groups, Amazon reviewers, and the Common Reader.

Ars brevis

STEPHEN BURT ON THE TWENTIETH CENTURY'S FINEST SHORT POEMS

I want to start thinking about this century's shortest good poems by way of two very long books: the Library of America's brand-new *American Poetry, the Twentieth Century*, Volumes I and II (hereafter, *LoA*). Restricted to poets born before 1913, the pair of black hardbacks cover all that five editors (Robert Hass, John Hollander, Carolyn Kizer, Nathaniel Mackey, Marjorie Perloff) could fit into just over 2000 pages. Within them, one finds *The Waste Land*, and Bessie Smith's blues lyrics, and obscure Dadaists' nonsense poetry, and Vachel Lindsay (an American Liverpool poet of sorts, sixty years *avant la lettre*), and Langston Hughes and Robert Frost, and obscure poems which seem to have influenced Frost, and Marianne Moore and William Carlos Williams, and the Williams-ish poets known as the Objectivists. In the last category belongs Charles Reznikoff (1894-1976), a lawyer best known for the very long poem *Testimony*; this anthology reveals him instead as a master of very short poems, poems conveying not just a scene or image but a psychology, sometimes even a politics. This one neither has nor needs a title:

> In the shop, she, her mother, and grandmother,
> thinking at times of women at windows in still
>   streets,
> or women reading, a glow on resting hands.

The trio in the shop (perhaps garment workers) envy the hands of women who don't have to work with their hands – who can afford to stay up late, or to keep the light on, simply to read. Here's another untitled poem:

> A grove of small trees, branches thick with berries,
> and within it, the constant twitter of birds.
> The trees of the park this cold windy day
> for want of leaves
> are hung with paper – strips of dirty paper.

Like Williams, Reznikoff knew how to track the sightlines of an observer, stopping a poem at the first detail that could render a sentence minatory or ironic, or balance its conflicting parts.

The famous Imagistes of 1914-15 – led by Ezra Pound – sought (as their anthology put it) "poetry that is hard and clear", devoted to concentration – in practice, short poems, and poems visual first and last. Reznikoff's poems could count as imagist if they had to; they can resist long interpretive moves, or reward them. Besides the ever-anthologized 'In a Station of the Metro', Pound's own best imagist poem might be 'L'Art, 1910':

> Green arsenic smeared on an egg-white cloth,
> Crushed strawberries! Come, let us feast our eyes.

How much does it matter that arsenic can kill you? Does it matter that the colors make up an Italian flag?

Imagism – and its distinguished ancestors in classical Chinese poetry, Japanese tanka and haiku – names one tradition of short poems; "epigram" names another line of descent. The American poet J. V. Cunningham (1911-85) – another *LoA* beneficiary – devoted most of his career to epigrams, stern or salty, mordant or fiercely moralized. Like his mentor Yvor Winters, Cunningham found the core of poetry in the act of considered judgement. Unlike Winters, Cunningham sought out dark humor: he gave one view of an entire era in 'They':

> Of all the gods that were
> Remains one deity:
> *Who do they think they are?*
> *They can't do this to me.*

Even older than the Roman epigrams Cunningham cherished is the surviving corpus of Greek lyric. Canadian poet Anne Carson's skill with very short poems has emerged from her classical learning. Her writings on lyric and epic – on Sappho, and Simonides, and Stesichoros – suggest how archaeologically-retrieved fragments of poems become of necessity, for belated interpreters, whole poems of a special kind. We enjoy, in them, a sense of the unfinished, and we invoke experiences for which fragmentariness stands: broken-off encounters, unanswerable queries, unfinished lives. Carson's adaptations of Greek lyric often take advantage of fragmentation, as in these two slices of 'Mimnermos: The Brainsex Paintings' (from Carson's 1995 *Plainwater*):

fr. 16
> *Troubled.*
> ...always the hard word box they wanted.

fr. 23
> *Why does motion sadden him?*
> ...a lame man knows the sex act best...

Antiquity left us Greek lyric, Roman epigram, Li Po, Japanese haiku; the nineteenth century adds the Blakean sentence, Wordsworth's Lucy poems, much of Dickinson, and some distinguished epigrammatists (Coleridge, Landor, Housman). All these (and more) create a sort of continuum: from it, weirder, hybrid, very short poems have emerged. W.S. Merwin's 'Elegy' reads, in its entirety:

> Who would I show it to

What more compact version of grief has there been? If that poem is neither epigram nor image, Yeats' 'The Nineteenth Century and After' manages to be both:

> Though the great song return no more
> There's keen delight in what we have:
> The rattle of pebbles on the shore
> Under the receding wave.

Vivid enough in themselves, the wave-and-rattle also imply that no more ought to be stated – moderns' "keen delight", pressed only a little, would turn into dejection as Romanticism finally wore itself out.

All these poems contain their own rationale for being as small as they are – they suggest either that the one picture they give says it all, or that a speaker is too choked-up to say more. And here is a general rule for very short poems: the poem has to use – to "foreground", even – its brevity, just as it uses other properties, like diction or rhyme. Brevity can simply mean strong closure: it works that way in poems about closure, or about aftermath. Patric Dickinson's 'Forgiveness' makes its compactness a sign that a quarrel, a day, a fire, and perhaps even a marriage are over and done with:

> A candle in a cold house
> Nibbled by a cold mouse:
> Come, Forgiveness, bell the cat
> Light the wick, let that be that.

What other properties can brevity have? One is *tact*; another is its opposite, *emphasis*. The very short poem can also become an *epitaph*. The earliest known Greek lyric poems (Carson has noted) originated as epitaphs. Carson's latest series of short poems, from *Men in the Off Hours*, model themselves on epitaphs: each claims (however obliquely) to summarize or justify a life. 'Epitaph: Zion' seems to remember a suicide:

> Murderous little world once our objects had gazes.
>   Our lives
>   Were fragile, the wind
> Could dash them away. Here lies the refugee breather
>   Who drank a bowl of elsewhere.

Akin to epitaph, but friendlier, is the short poem summing up a long life: one is Robert Crawford's poem about the Biblical matriarch 'Sarah':

> My husband's a bachle. I love him.
> A hundred, his penis is a rag.
>
> Listening to foreigners, I laughed at the tentflap.
> He squints at me now, a nodding camel,
> Dry lips suspicious with faith.
>
> What should I do, a woman of ninety,
> Squalling like a baby at this new mirage
> Beyond the tent door, finding how
> God has made me for laughter?

The American poet A. R. Ammons specializes in very long (book-length) and in very short poems; the latter assemble in *The Really Short Poems of A. R. Ammons* (1990). Ammons likes to think about scale: he enjoys the *contrast* between giant (metaphysical or cosmological) topics and small utterances, a contrast short poems almost automatically provide. The first and second halves of his 'Immoderation' seem to state, in two versions, the same truth:

> If something is too
> big, enlarging it
> may correct it:
> a skinny thing
> acquires great force
> pushed next to nothing.

Along with brevity and finality comes implicit *unity*, which helps the short poem mimic, in its motion, one scene, one object, or one action. Ammons mimics all three in 'Small Song':

> The reeds give
> way to the
>
> wind and give
> the wind away

The short poem of mimesis – where the poem's progress, its structure of breath, pace and pause, try to resemble the process the poem describes – became a specialty of William Carlos Williams', in poems like 'The Term' and 'The Maneuver'. In the latter, "two starlings, just before alighting",

> turned in the air together
> and landed backwards!
> that's what got me – to
> face into the wind's teeth.

Visual mimesis may not even require motion: another Objectivist, Louis Zukofsky (1904-78), captured a kind of stillness in his 'All of December Toward New Year's':

> Not the branches
> half in shadow
>
> But the length
> of each branch
>
> Half in shadow
>
> As if it had snowed
> on each upper half

A short poem's descriptive completeness can also suggest a *caption*. Verse-tags once accompanied the visual emblems in Renaissance emblem-books; modern short poems more often behave like captions for photographs, as in Randall Jarrell's 'The Sign':

> Having eaten their mackerel, drunk their milk,
> They lie like two skeins of embroidery silk Asleep in
> the glider. The child repeats, "It's *such* a pity!"
> And paints on a piece of beaverboard, FREE KITTY.

Paul Muldoon may be the most versatile poet alive in his use of very short forms: his *Kerry Slides* (1995) consists of short verses paired to photographs they seem to describe. One couplet makes high comedy out of sheep dip:

> This cobalt-quiffed ewe among the fuchsia's
> part blue-rinsed Grandmama, part Sid Vicious.

Another caption-poem uses syncopation to overturn the implicit seriousness of memorial poetry:

> Twilight. The graveyard at Annascaul.
> Its six-foot-high wall
> is hardly about
> to keep anyone in, and no one out.

Lavinia Greenlaw's 'Three' might also serve to caption a photograph; such a photo would be an extreme close-up, disturbing – like the poem, like the gesture the poem describes – in how close it comes:

> Your shaved head on my thigh
> evokes a third thing,
> the quorum or casting vote of us
>
> – as Aquinas struggled to fit
> the perpetual quality of hair
> into his logic of resurrection
>
> so, wanting more for us,
> you subtract another millimetre
> from the setting of the razor's edge.

Aided by its brevity, Greenlaw's poem describes the tiny but ineradicable distance between people in terms of fine hairs, scholastics' fine hair-splitting, the breadth and depth of one layer of live skin.

If one sort of small poem hangs on a single image, another kind gathers a set of tokens, a *collection* of objects or terms which summarize a whole life. This sort of small poem can be especially moving when the life thus summarized seems more restricted than most. Here (and in *LoA*) is Lorine Niedecker's (1903-1970) one-sentence summary of her rural family:

> The clothesline post is set
> yet no totem-carvings distinguish the Niedecker tribe
> from the rest; every seventh day they wash;
> worship sun; fear rain, their neighbors' eyes;
> raise their hands from ground to sky,
> and hang or fall by the whiteness of their all.

The "tribe" have been – no, have *almost* been – reduced to their laundry: could our lives, too, admit of such quiet summary? The mordancy of epigram, the effect of summary or collection, and the sense that the poet wants an emphatic ending (to a poem or to a human relation) all inform the short poems of Michael Hofmann. His 'June' becomes a short poem about writing in short forms, and a short bit of (appalled) nostalgia about a love affair no part of which could last long:

> Short forms. Lines, sentences, *bonmots*.
> Part of an afternoon, a truncated night,
> interstitial evening. Rarely a paragraph
> or stanza ('room'), never a day and a day and a day...
> Half-pints and double-deckers, the river, the
>   cemetery,
> always on the *qui vive* (why, ourselves of course!) –
> our honeymoon epic in illicit installments.

A short poem can hold one image, or half a dozen, but it almost always constitutes a single *speech-act*: as such, it can sum up a speaker's psychology at a particular instant. Merwin's 'Elegy' makes one example; Langston Hughes' 'Evil' (also in *LoA*) makes another:

> Looks like what drives me crazy
> Don't have no effect on you –
> But I'm gonna keep on at it
> Till it drives you crazy too

Robert Creeley's 'Ambition' slaps together a set of weak verbs, almost stuttering as it compiles its triple rhythms, and miming its speaker's shyness:

> Couldn't guess it,
> couldn't be it –
>
> wasn't ever
> there then. Won't
>
> come back, don't
> want it.

– two sentences, five verb-phrases, one disintegrating dimeter rhythm, one speech-act. A single speech-act, in turn, can stop short for emphasis, or for added authority, or even out of sheepishness. Auden in his last years wrote an astonishing array of haiku and tanka: each of the good ones give the form's natural fleetingness a different turn. Some come off as shamblingly authoritative:

> Few can remember
> clearly when innocence came
> to a sudden end,
> the moment at which we ask
> for the first time: *Am I loved?*

Others are touching and personal in the extreme –

> Unable to speak Icelandic,
> he helped instead
> to do the dishes.

Who hasn't been, in that sense, to Auden's Iceland? The single speech act rejoins the classical epigram in poems conceived as sharp quips: in this category falls Ammons' comically symmetrical 'Their Sex Life' – "One failure on / Top of another". Thom Gunn's most famous quip is 'Jamesian': "Their relationship consisted / In discussing if it existed". Such quick sayings or comments work well in series – Ben Jonson, and Cunningham, numbered theirs; Auden often printed several strung together. The serial sentences of Frank O'Hara's 'Lines for the Fortune Cookies' exist on the comic fringes of permanent utterance –

> You should wear white more often – it becomes
>   you..
> The next person to speak to you will have a very
>   intriguing proposal to make.
> A lot of people in this room wish they were you.

O'Hara's fortune-cookies remind us of how much what we get out of a poem depends on what we're able to put in, and on what we are asked to put in – for example, by a title. John Ashbery's one-line poems (from his 1979 book *As We Know*) use comic disproportion to make poems whose effects lie mostly in what we see before we reach the poem:

> OUT OVER THE BAY THE RATTLE OF
>   FIRECRACKERS
> And in the adjacent waters, calm.

All these are kinds of very short poems, different ways to use the potential meanings of brevity, the power small bits of poetic language can have. To them might be added another kind of short poem, one which hasn't been explored enough yet: this is the answer to an implicit question, a question implied if not posed by the title, and one which startles or overwhelms or discomfits the speaker, or else prompts a witty reply. Carson and Ashbery and Muldoon have all come close to writing such poems. I leave an exercise for the reader; Is there somewhere a title, or a context, which could make a whole poem out of "No thank you, I'd rather walk?"

NOTE: U.K. readers can find more Reznikoff, more Zukofsky, and more Niedecker in Andrew McAllister's 1996 Bloodaxe anthology *The Objectivists*.

TWO POEMS BY STEPHEN BURT

HOROSHINKE

Entrained to the least scent,
Distractable as an ancient radio,
Why do you keep that distance and no other? Why do you please
Yourself and cover your unruly ground

By sweeping a paw across it, pulling back
One tensor at a time, so that the roots
Of the claws you have
No practical use for show? What happiness is

For you is as hard to learn as it is for
Us, yet you have learned; you sleep on your back,
Showing your furred ribs to three out of four
Elements.   Why should you wink

When irritable, or scowl, then yawn and stretch
Out in a backwards saddle shape when pleased?
What number are you dialing?   As if a ruse
To join the world of act to mere behavior,

You slice at yourself in the mirror of the day . . .
O find the other kitten, or else wrestle
For weeks, until your gift of speech returns:
Walk across us each night. Sharpen your tracks.

LIKE A WRECK

Flaunting your useless knowledge has failed you again,
Though it was all they had taught you. Worse yet,
Those self-demotions had always worked
In emergencies before; now they seemed about
To succumb to a Coriolis-cum-Peter
Principle: each fact sinks
Until you have to dredge it up and get
Away with it before it can trouble
The ruffled surface of the dream you share.

So once again, they've run you out of
Town on a toy train. It all seems pleasant:
These clapboard shurbs and candybox pastels
Part where the heathers wave back at us. Do they know?
A folded hillside saves snow; it shines like diapers,
Parts and shows
The larch you noticed the last time you wet your pants.
It was a Thursday. The tall teacher cleared the room
As sunlight shocked the prurient glass doors . . .

The tracks ahead continue to choke and spurt.
When were you alive? New shoes won't help.
Neither will asking the right questions. Maybe a ring . . .
To stay in your present tense, and keep your promise,
We'll have to clear these girders off you first.

ANTHONY LAWRENCE
THE DRIVE-IN

The drive-in screen was a transparency
of epic proportions, the speaker posts and boxes
unmarked headstones scratchy with dialogue,

the most distant of them unvisited and framed
by closely planted pines. I always expected the screen to rise,
its animated, two-storey-high faces sliding down

like drowners beyond the fixative of dusk
and the ropework of projector beams, leaving a wire fence,
weeds and the eyes of nightbirds – a dark billboard

for adventure, horror and love stalled over Sydney.
It was outside this parking lot for parking teens
who came in the boots of friends' cars

or under blankets like angular, breathing luggage
that we stopped to touch and taste each other.
In the back of a Datsun, we entered cramped positions

we would later resume and extend, in comfort,
when older, on beds at home. I remember looking up
to find you watching the movie, or parts of it,

through the open window and the pines, breathing slowly
as you responded by saying yes or moving yourself
against me. We took turns and stayed for hours,

our faces gleaming with streetlight and what our bodies made.
There was a scene involving an aeroplane
and a mountainside that ended in blue flames.

I was about to mention this, when you found a place
I responded to and then responded to,
the flames going to water as the scene dissolved

Nude Formalism

by Jules Mann

An Anthology of New (American) Poets
Edited by Lisa Jarnot, Leonard Schwartz
and Chris Stroffolino
Talisman House, $21.95
ISBN 1 883689 61 9

ONE OF THE juicy side-effects of any collection but particularly of "new poets" is the opportunity to see what presses and magazines have been publishing these poets in the beginning stages of their career. In this case, it provides a glimpse of the rich territory of small press activity across America: O Books, Burning Deck, Granary Books, Avec, The Figures, Leave Books, Manic D. Press, Sun and Moon, o.blek editions, and of course Talisman House which published this collection entitled *An Anthology of New (American) Poet*s. A cross-section of magazines these poets have appeared in includes *First Intensity*, *mirage*, *Mass. Ave*, *Ploughshares*, *Sulfur*, *The Impercipient* and *Transfer*. And then there are the magazines the poets themselves edit: *Chain*, *Tender Buttons*, *Proliferation*, *Psalm 151*, *Clamour*, *The Transcendental Friend*, *Outpost Entropy*, *Skanky Possum*, *Tinfish*, *Aerial* and *Situation*.

The editors clarify that the writers in this anthology for the most part were born in the '60s (actually between 1958-1973) and have published one full collection of poetry. I would also comment that the '(American)' in the title need not be parenthetical, and that it's refreshing to see the writing of as many women as men.

Beth Anderson demonstrates a consistently powerful momentum within complex, often intuited levels of meaning:

> ...Though disembodied may feel like
> a familiar passage it must be observed that singing
> does echo
> both from one mythology of a large rumbling storm
> and from
> a morning opening into a crowded room. So quiet I
> could hear my ears ring.
>
> ('Alleged Original')

Lee Ann Brown contributes her sparse "Nude Formalism" style; Mary Burger her hilarious inner-character-within monologues, as well as poems and short treatises which manage to be either self-deprecatingly or casually intellectual. Somewhat disjunctive absurdism from Jordan Davis and accomplished visual/political work from Brenda Coultas, which at times verges on conceptual art, such as this passage from 'Diorama':

> One day I was out walking and came upon a small
> container of Janet Reno. She wears a nurse's cape
> and white starched hat. She wears enough white to
> pass for Elizabeth Dole. Janet is living in a box. She's
> in the shape of a tv. All the world is on my tv.
> World, get off my tv.

Thomas Sayers Ellis's traditional free verse style generates its own compelling rhythm:

> No fear. Every now and then, an uninformed god
> Will walk in, bear witness, mistake Kangol
> For halo, all those names for unwanted bodies
> Being called home, arms raised to testify, waving
> From side to side, fists flying like bullets, bullets
> Like fists.
>
> ('A Baptist Beat')

Benjamin Friedlander contributes perhaps the most formal style, including (gasp!) end-rhymes and an abundance of language-play. Drew Gardner's interesting work strikes me as someone simultaneously translating while minutely observing; I particularly enjoyed his not-just-about-computer poems such as 'The Source Log': "the current to create / or series of nested source / or store without // entering others / appears along the window, turned / the car around / to an egret standing in the ditch".

I'm happy to report that prose poems are still alive and well, as evidenced by Renee Gladman's 'ARLEM', a collection of vivid poems keenly delineating the complexities of desire, race and poetics in a gripping story with a very individual voice.

Yuri Hospodar's contemporary pop-political poems contain overtones of oral tradition that resonates well with Mark Nowak's chanting, oral-style of mythical poetry. Chris Stroffollino veers close to contemporary beat poetry, showing deft rhythm and a hip hop gush of language.

Susan M. Schultz contributes a heady mix of introspective philosophical argument whereas Lisa

Jarnot takes the reader on more of a journalistic urban travelogue. Then along comes the intelligent, hard-hitting poetry of Candace Kaucher with great titles ('Virginibus Puerisque', 'Molecular Viscosity', 'Ex Post Facto God') and deep imagination. This stanza comes from 'Swallowed Opinions but Good Ones':

> It's a black hole bulimic on a diet of emptiness
> with just the demon sided page flapping in
> an unfettered step to the next day's affairs,
> a sad box of carnivals accustomed to shining
> brightly in the lap of commodity.

I was less taken with Heather Ramsdell's work included here (not up to her usual penetration of language, and though the selections are long they aren't urgent); Bill Luoma's classical style contrasts sharply with much of the other work, which is no bad thing; Peter Gizzi and Judith Goldman lend their more mature (and to my ear slightly less exciting) voices to the collection. Elizabeth Willis demonstrates an intriguingly spare, mythic poetry, and Juliana Spahr spins a long piece of closely observed particulars: nuances of Gertrude Stein.

On to the more highly-charged imaginations of Kimberly Lyons, Mark McMorris and Jeffrey McDaniel, the latter showing a fine ear for the humour of the modern world. Jennifer Moxley with her very poetic and philosophical language, similar in some ways to Pam Rehm though Rehm plays much more on the musicality of internal rhyme.

One of the most stunning poets in this collection is Clare Needell. Spare, beautiful and so tightly constructed you soon begin to implicitly trust where you are being taken. In its entirety her work seems to describe meditations on space, flight, the body... yet also containing complex layers of visual art, consciousness, scientific principles and new definitions.

> Comes. Uncolored
> because light
> exceeds lines
> of body.
> ('Another and Another')

> Ribbons of it unfold,
> cause air to sway,
> cause the radiance
> that should be "bird".
> ('Space Remains')

> There is no deciding shape,
> image. It moves in, out.
> Is there and turning.
> ('But For Now')

Having said that, in a completely different manner but no less stunning is Hoa Nguyen, whose work demonstrates a spacious breadth of style, creative play with syntax and absolutely logical and commanding spaces (breath stops). From 'Surrogate Houses':

> Tension's tinny motive to locate. Action value.
> It's a click it's done it's undone it's a loud cord
> according to attitude   longitude   device.
> ...
> You seek   stung by the sun   your solar
> plexus flexed   breathing composed for a blow.

Leonard Schwartz, whose language dances:

> Each flare of perception
> a lonely peregrination
> of the formless into form
>
> A fulgurating synthesis
> arched over a rush of broken bones
> ('Pages from an Imaginary Escape')

With her unusual use of language, Eleni Sikelianos's poetry has an otherworldly essence, while Rod Smith's poems read like sax improvisations:

> Blowsey boys, bubble O
>   The tiger of a growth
> A hill full – a hole full
>   is scanty easily scattered
> All of a row
>   ('In Memory of my Theories')

In a similar vein, Edwin Torres's inventive work stretches, decapitates and reassembles words while maintaining an eerily clear sense of vision (a sort of adult Dr. Seuss). "Umbilical ribbons. Patrinnical trimming. A quarter-inch of / soundstuffs, particled rough audicals, bound oracal" ('Let's go Swimming in the key of C').

As a whole, the collection refreshes with its breadth of language and variation of styles and it is truly exciting to get a glimpse of the 30-something generation's writing.

THE CLASSIC POEM

SELECTED BY DENNIS O'DRISCOLL

FOR A LONG time, English-language poetry readers knew Czesław Miłosz as the translator of Zbigniew Herbert and anthologist of *Post-War Polish Poetry* but not as a major poet in his own right. Similarly, Robert Hass is recognised outside of America as the translator of Czesław Miłosz rather than as an original master (America's finest contemporary poet, in my opinion). Exploring California last May, I suddenly realised that I was not in Marin County but in Hass Country. The name-boards of small Bay Area towns were prompts for the titles of his poems: 'Graveyard at Bolinas', 'At Stinson Beach', 'The Apple Trees at Olema', 'Meditation at Lagunitas'...

Implicit in 'Meditation at Lagunitas' is the conviction that – whatever philosophers or literary theorists may contend concerning the gulf between word and world – the human practice is to press on regardless and to achieve communication not just through words but also by means of rhythm, image and body language. Hass transcends the barriers of language to apprehend the world sensuously, writing in the poem, 'Spring': "when I said 'The limits of my language / are the limits of my world', you laughed. / We spoke all night in tongues, / in fingertips, in teeth". Far from reducing words to the intellectual equivalent of a San Francisco fog ("talking this way, everything dissolves"), he uses them as a repository of memories ("I remember so much") which resonate and ripple and ramify. In Hass's bittersweet poetry, lines of communication remain permanently open.

ROBERT HASS
MEDITATION AT LAGUNITAS

All the new thinking is about loss.
In this it resembles all the old thinking.
The idea, for example, that each particular erases
the luminous clarity of a general idea. That the clown-
faced woodpecker probing the dead sculpted trunk
of that black birch is, by his presence,
some tragic falling off from a first world
of undivided light. Or the other notion that,
because there is in this world no one thing
to which the bramble of *blackberry* corresponds,
a word is elegy to what it signifies.
We talked about it late last night and in the voice
of my friend, there was a thin wire of grief, a tone
almost querulous. After a while I understood that,
talking this way, everything dissolves: *justice,
pine, hair, woman, you* and *I*. There was a woman
I made love to and I remembered how, holding
her small shoulders in my hands sometimes,

I felt a violent wonder at her presence
like a thirst for salt, for my childhood river
with its island willows, silly music from the pleasure boat,
muddy places where we caught the little orange-silver fish
called *pumpkinseed*. It hardly had to do with her.
Longing, we say, because desire is full
of endless distances, I must have been the same to her.
But I remember so much, the way her hands dismantled bread,
the thing her father said that hurt her, what
she dreamed. There are moments when the body is as numinous
as words, days that are the good flesh continuing.
Such tenderness, those afternoons and evenings,
saying *blackberry, blackberry, blackberry.*

From *Praise* by Robert Hass. Copyright © 1990, by Robert Hass. Reprinted by arrangement with HarperCollins Publishers, Inc.

Cosmopolibackofbeyondism

BY ROBERT CRAWFORD

COSMOPOLIBACKOFBEYONDISM is a creed with a wink in it. Poetry's obsessions – love, death, God, sound, silence – travel across times and cultures; nothing could be more cosmopolitan. At the same time, verse is a marginal act, operating way out at the back of beyond, at the limits of what can be said. Its centrality and marginality are bonded.

Every poem is an island. To get to a poem requires sailing out from the mainland of routine language. Some poems are close to shore, others much further away; on every island it is possible to feel remote and at home. A poem is defined by the rugged shore of its right-hand margin, cutting it off from prose. Yet just as any poem-island has the tang of the back of beyond, it has, too, aspects, shared speech-forms, political shapes, faiths, which link it to other places. All poems are connected, most simply through the shared cosmopolis of verse.

'Verse' means "turning". Some of the ancients likened verse to the movement of oxen as they ploughed a furrow, then wheeled round to plough the next. In this sense every maker of verse is a ploughman poet, breaking open a field of silence. On its little journey, each verse line leads silence into sound, sound into silence. Unlike prose, verse marks a birth and death between every line and the next. Any line, at its centre, its wee acoustic cosmopolis, is moving from margin to margin, sea to sea. It is alert to the back of beyond.

Line-breaks are the fundamental act of patterning in a poem, the one on which all other patterns depend. To write in two-line stanzas readily heightens this; there's not just a turn from line to line, but every second line there's a bigger intrusion of the margin, a firth flowing into the poem. Poems should be read aloud, their margins heeded, but even in silence the breaking of lines constitutes the life of verse. Borges wrote, "Beyond the rhythm of a line of verse, its typographical arrangement serves to tell the reader that it's poetic emotion, not information or rationality, that he or she should expect". The poetic line signals a kind of magical interference with the prose world of daily transactions.

Yet, precisely because poetry involves a playing

with expectations, it is a gleeful thing to make the informational part of poetic emotion. Opposites attract. The enduring, backofbeyondish, sacred aspects of verse must be fused with, though not lost in, the available language and textures of the age. The textures of our era's language are informational.

In that sense we have all become cosmopolitan, but unless poets can also dwell at the back of beyond, they cannot respond to the full spectrum of words. Bound up with international, cosmopolitan English lingo are colorations peculiar to local microclimates. Dialect, backofbeyondisms, jargons of science and information must all be heard. Poets should be simultaneously central and marginal, to such a degree that it is no longer clear which is which.

One of the most revealing lines of English poetry is Donne's iambic pentameter

> I wonder by my troth, what thou, and I

which places the self, the "I", at the margins, at the alpha and omega of the line. "My troth" at the line's heart is not really the central "troth" of betrothal, but, revealingly, something throwaway. Centre and margins have changed place; the ego, so crucial to this poem, is also peripheral, way out at each end of the line. Less egotistically, and more movingly, Ben Jonson opens a poem

> Farewell, thou child of my right hand, and joy;

where, subtly but significantly, the first syllable tolls more loudly than usual in an iambic pentameter. In sound and feeling this line to Jonson's dead young son is weighed down at start and finish. In each case these poets let their line-ends resonate into the margins beyond, so that the extremities are at least as important as the centre. The lines are acoustically devolved.

Patron saints of Cosmopolibackofbeyondism are many. Hugh MacDiarmid is one of them. Developing the cosmological imagination of his great Scots and English verse while living in Montrose, then on Whalsay in the Shetlands, he fused vernacular and highbrow, galaxy and doorstep. He presented his vision of a new Scottish modernist poetry to the local YMCA. He saw the impossible, then did it.

More and more as the margins and centres of language, politics, and gender are smudged, Cosmopolibackofbeyondism beckons. To sound its music is to love all language, remaining true to our electronic global present at the same time as keeping faith with local, theological, vernacular, and aureate values. The balance between verse's newness and antiquity is as necessary and impossible as its juggling between centre and margin. Ultimately, poetry thrives on impossibilities and takes them as its most urgent language, its way of saying something new or anew. Philosophy, journalism, and "the media" ultimately distrust the unique medium of verse. They want to erode its all-seeing, mediumistic uniqueness, paraphrasing it in terms more packagably familiar. Poetry, so central to human experience, always tends to gravitate beyond the end of the line. The poet winkingly truncates Wittgenstein: "About which we cannot speak we must".

Taken from *Strong Words: Modern Poets on Modern Poetry* (eds W. N. Herbert and Matthew Hollis), to be published by Bloodaxe in September, featuring 35 of the 20th-century's most challenging statements about poetry, with 35 newly commissioned pieces.

TWO POEMS BY KATHLEEN STEWART
DOWN BELOW

They have made a veil for me!
Sewn with the needles from some bobbled tree.
When will they accept I am not coming back?
I cannot be dragged like this
from one world to the next.
The light hurts my skin like a rain of pins.
When will they accept I cannot come home?
All the burden of their prayers for me
like stones I must carry.
So, I am dead to them?
Let them bury me.

Must I rise, every year, to reassure them that I live?
Does this reassure them that they will not die?
An annual letter would suffice me – and I
would pen a brief reply. While here, every year,
the same pointlessly good news – marriages, births –
the same cycle of calamities.
But we must celebrate, celebrate!
Here is the sun!
Remember? Birds fly and children leap
and here is the sea!

How they praise the sky with their buildings.
How they would climb up into it.
At night, the ropes of emeralds, rubies, pearls.
The processional lights that hover on their roads.
The great silver birds, splayed elephants.
The carriages that hurtle themselves
along the spokes of spiders' webs, the wheels.
This ceaseless trawling after sensation!
They call it living?

In my world, all that they fear,
all that they spend their lifetimes trying to deny
slithers over me.
I want for nothing, down below.

389

The monstrous bus descends, wings unfurled –
my deliverance

Me and my bones hobble aboard
an unlikely pair

Bones, well-known hoofers
Me, more tragedy-prone

Pain sits patiently beside me
clamps a hand upon my knee

Only wait, I tell myself
or pain tells me

Oh, but he's a slow bus! Slow he winds
through houses trellised with iron vines

Stealthy creeps he by the shopping mall
losing time –

all the time pocketed, profligate
in that joyous steady rush uphill –

as an old woman winds up wool
and then unwinds it.

TWO POEMS BY JEFF CLARK
LIKE CATS COMING OUT OF LOCKS

(– Will Alexander)

Channeled for a periled Sandy
after a snifter of her spirits at the intersection of 2nd & C
in a memory   *Like cats coming out of clocks*
Three seconds so a voice say
Like cats coming out of clocks
to fly so our eyes never find you again
from the Golden Gate to a range of saline
Like cats coming out of clocks
Or mistaken seers now gone foresaw a drop in a closet
Like cats coming out of clocks
But a parallel barrel obliterates a pearl
A parallel barrel resonates a pool in a marvelous garden
that dries and leaves alkali
Like cats coming out of clocks
You saw a lily tilt when you were ill
Like cats coming out of clocks
Or a hummingbird struck from the air in Marysville
You were trying to defend petals from the hovering hoses
that surrounded the loud canal
Objects of the hallway will rot
But you will prey on the jubilant voices
Like cats coming out of clocks
First kill the Princes who sells this memory of an hour
back to the memory's owner
Like cats coming out of clocks
whose friend's hours were sold
to a rust orphanage in a fragrant orange grove
untended since the first breath
of the barrel or the mouth of the girl
who strew the seeds
or strung the string through wet beads

A CHOCOLATE AND A MANTIS

The phosphorous cheeks of an ailing jester fallen that day
from an alien haze over jade lanes
to blades arrayed in ribboned mazes
created to flay a dilated spirit hole
He was a chaotic boy with phosphorous cheeks
and a glistening sphinctral sanctity
a purple fallen alloy of a Medium
and a Gigola to sleeps
He was white waste of nebula-scented hours
fallen that day an alien length
to a place of stale rain and that day
to crawl crying to the side
was to harvest no more eggs of fantasy strewn out horizontally
and found by following a hare that could be a guide or a lie in fur
He was hideous when he ate the eggs, and in a trance
a chocolate and a mantis sat on his thigh
and said that Even broken or swollen
hysterical inside long boxes or on wires
or swallowing gray fay lures
to take and decompose both your lapel rose and the hose that fed it
you must offer a mantis your hand, a chocolate your tongue
then never again ill use or even dream to curate
fake faces or oases or their words

And sometimes you rejoice because you dream
and are engaged with a wet bottom
but dreamless to find that your senses are weaker
and you could feel no cigarette or Ra
no tilting park or clef
but the chaos of a sac of cracked slides
and scales, sucked-to-death larks and stabbing swings
and you knew that if you could be a jester bred to beg dream for eggs
if you could see a Jesus singing from a tree his own father grew
so could you polish all of a cellar with spit
or hold the shined tile of your face to a suffocated street this Sunday
or sometimes to the crown of two real or often two envisioned thighs
blessed by suburban or country perfumes

because sometimes you contorted to kiss the side of a false staff
and you dreamt you were decomposing
were dooming your face

to have wanted to kiss a stick in a mirage
and not a marigold harem or a brown crown
You saw madness was to love a lady muezzin you extracted from a tale
of manmade everglades in which masquerading ladies
play and get jauntily sprayed from the pram of a naked parader
because sometimes your face tasted of the taint of those papers of escape
and psychic counts dictated your fainting or what you would trust

Because sometimes you reclined so mistily on the wet lips of states
so shimmeringly on states
that a spectre slid up a gold or silver surface
you never leveled until it possessed and emptied you
and now escapes to exist in other ethers

because what is to be burned
is equally unpresent in your urns and blurs.

TWO POEMS BY ELLEN HINSEY
ON THE LIFE OF DECAY

Enmeshed in each moment – the green river of lichen
    Advances, undoes, the kingdom of surety;

      There – in a basin of darkness – below the edge
        Of light-level, where shadows cover wood's

Endurance – in that sea of air – in a jade air of undoing,
    Moisture robes each leaf left in the entombed

      Damp of a valley, under the crossed helix of
        Branches, crevasses alive with still water:

The trail of moss along the forest floor's dimensions,
    The mosaic of virus – inhabiting the cells –

      The incessant love of parasites, turning in their
        Toil, under the tight screen of ivy's stars –

Or above, the parched length of an old branch, dangling;
    The air biting, tunneling, in its feast of removal –

      Up on the hillside, the gale's caress chastening

     The rock face, seeking out with its brutal hand

The boiled surface of rust on the junked empty wagon,
  Bending a hinge as it swings into an empty berth:

    Whittling the roofs thatch, lifting the smoke of dry rot
      In waves, hammering the headland's old profile –

Until it lifts to observe lands gullied and bared; surveys fans
  Of sand run by rain, beat by sun – watches as

    Sodden soil, weight of earth once held in mass,
      Brings down hills suddenly to the mouth of the sea –

Here in each moment – water's endless song of erosion,
  And the terrible attack of the wind's undertow:

    Yes, the fast building crescendo, the vast knowledge
      Amassing, the return and holy rebuilding –

        Of the great, the final, temple of air.

ON VARIETIES OF FLIGHT

There, in the air – traceless blue – arena of circuits
  And saunters, some rise with difficulty

    While others lift buoyant, tack of tail turned
      Westward – take wide air under their keel,

And sprint, shoot and sail up to where, in invisible
  Gyres they revolve tropical or northern,
  Spreading their full breadth to survey the scene,
    Their prey hidden in land folded and patched;

Others, tail-sure tuck and dive, fall in a single tear,
  Against a stony silhouette of hill; others

    In wind jibe and yaw, storm-wise, head into
      Air as prows take the jab and flack of waves –

But some are threaded by thin parachute, line of silk,
    They soar only when bidden, cross a width

        Of draft, but hang when the wind is becalmed
            And suspended; still others come from deeper

Hues – leap into air as if seeking a higher realm,
    Where hidden stars crown a miraculous

        Dome of blue – fly on their fins, and their short
            Leap is the curve of Noah's colored arc:

Still for others, flight is trammeled – rooted, as fires lift
    Only in sparks, but are held fast to their

Flames; and sound flies blindly over distance,
    But cannot renew the force of its thrust;

Sight sweeps and tempers rise; tall grasses bend and
    Rumors mount; winds wind over, as insects

    Hover, and stars speed free under frail falling
        Night, while fleet tongues tell their tales –

And Knowledge – poor earth-bound ember – sails,
    But fails to ignite.

A SECOND LOOK

His damned hoobla-hoobla-hoobla-how

JUSTIN QUINN ON THE POETRY OF WALLACE STEVENS

WALLACE STEVENS NEVER quite caught on in Britain and Ireland. It might be because English publication took so long to come (Eliot, when belatedly redressing the situation, was said to have thought Stevens already had an English publisher), but then again it wasn't really until the publication of his *Collected Poems* in 1954 that he received wide recognition in the U.S. Thirty-six years on, Malcolm Bradbury and Richard Ruland in their survey of American literature reckoned that if his influence on proceeding generations of writers was anything to go by, then Stevens is one of the most important figures in the literature of his time. I was recently in the U.S. completing a book on his work and was amazed to see how different the reactions were to the research I was engaged in: in Ireland, mention of the book was something of a conversation-stopper; whereas I remember one evening with some young American poets in Boston in which it became the occasion for a long and animated discussion about his poetry. Quite simply, Stevens matters to American poets in a way he has never done for British or Irish – for the British, Auden is most likely to play this role, and for the Irish, Yeats. Edna Longley talks of his "imaginative autoeroticism"; and even Donald Davie, a critic with such broad American sympathies, has curiously little to say about him. For Sean O'Brien in 'Reading Stevens in the Bath', he's an opportunity to kick up some parodic suds:

> It is Newcastle at evening. It is far
> From the furnished banks of the coaly Tyne
> But close beside the hidden and infernal banks
>
> Of the unutterable Ouseburn. Howay. It cries
> Its native cry, this poisoned soup of prawns.
> Howay. The evil river sings....

One of the poems that O'Brien is parodying here is 'The House Was Quiet and the World Was Calm', and it's interesting that the same poem was used by a very different poet, this time American, to introduce a book of essays on the relations between poetry and politics. For such a ideologically committed poet as Adrienne Rich, one would have expected Stevens's work to represent a culpable poetic escapism. But the terms of her engagement are more subtle:

> You are drawn in not because this is a description of your world, but because you begin to be reminded of your own desire and need, because the poem is not about integration and fulfillment, but about the desire (*That makes thy sleepes so broken*) for those conditions. You listen, if you do, not simply to the poem, but to a part of you reawakened by the poem, momentarily made aware, a need both emotional and physical, that can for a moment be affirmed there.

For Rich, the poem provokes a hushed, hieratic commentary, and this seriousness is shared by other American poets, most strongly by Jorie Graham, perhaps the finest recent scion of the Stevensian tradition. But while Graham is drawn to the ambitious metaphysics of his work, it would seem that for her his slapstick aspects (which O'Brien picks up on so well) don't appear on the radar.

Whose is the real Stevens then? Well, they're both right. One of reasons that he continues to delight me is his amazing ability in the space of a few lines to move from the vatic to the humorous and back again. A good example of this is canto III of "It Must Be Abstract" from "Notes Toward a Supreme Fiction":

> The poem refreshes life so that we share,
> For a moment, the first idea... It satisfies
> Belief in an immaculate beginning
>
> And sends us, winged by an unconscious will,

To an immaculate end. We move between these
    points:
From that ever-early candor to its late plural

And the candor of them is the strong exhilaration
Of what we feel from what we think, of thought
Beating in the heart, as if blood newly came,

An elixir, an excitation, a pure power.
The poem, through candor, brings back a power
    again
That gives a candid kind to everything.

We say: At night an Arabian in my room,
With his damned hoobla-hoobla-hoobla-how,
Inscribes a primitive astronomy

Across the unscrawled forms the future casts
And throws his stars around the floor. By day
The wood-dove used to chant his hoobla-hoo

And still the grossest iridescence of ocean
Howls hoo and rises and howls hoo and falls.
Life's nonsense pierces us with strange relation.

The first four tercets are the kind of poetry about poetry that Longley gives out about. But it's hard to imagine a philosophical poetry that is more anchored in the motions and emotions that course through the body ("Beating in the heart, as if blood newly came, // An elixir, an excitation, a pure power"). The epigraph to an earlier poem goes: "The great interests of man: air and light, the joy of having a body, the voluptuousness of looking". The extent to which he is the chanticleer of these very "interests" is passed over in most criticism of Stevens. His joy in the physical aspect of things sponsors his more abstract meditations. In interview, Jorie Graham described him as "a poet so fully in the body, in his senses, and moving towards the conceptual and philosophical in order to complete himself". Also, coming back to the canto above, the political resonance of the sixth line in the American context (which turns *e pluribus unum* upside down), indicates that it's not just poems that Stevens is talking about, but *poeisis*, that is, any human making, be it political, religious, or aesthetic. A lot of his poetry is concerned not so much with the exhilarations and insights of the individual imagination, but with how the collective experiences and mediates them through culture. If the passage above were transposed into the first-person, it would be very different indeed.

And then, barging into all this comes the image of the Arabian jumping around the bedroom. This kind of comic exuberance is everywhere in his work, and what is curious is the way that it serves not to deflate the seriousness of his philosophising, but drive it on. Observe how the last line here returns to the contemplative mode of the canto's beginning, while keeping faith with all the hoo-ing which immediately preceded it. It is a kind of doubleness, a comic element in his unwillingness to reach for a profounder conclusion, as though, after his demanding and dextrous demonstration, he flops on the divan with a humorous whistle, and says platitudinously: "Isn't life strange?" The platitude is an excellent punchline precisely because of the true strangeness of the demonstration.

It remains unlikely that Stevens will ever matter in Britain. The dominant tradition, stretching from Hardy through Larkin to such contemporary practitioners as Thom Gunn, Carol Ann Duffy, Glyn Maxwell, and Sean O'Brien, is essentially grounded in dramatic narrative and unengaged by the type of philosophical interests that fuelled so much of Stevens's poetry. Also, I think British poets have no time for irony or humour that is not deflationary, and it is precisely this which animates Stevens's exhilarations and moments of the sublime. As for across the water, I remember how one senior Irish poet once asked me why 'The Auroras of Autumn' was ever written. And people ask me why I don't live in Ireland.

Recommended reading by and about Stevens

Milton J. Bates, *Wallace Stevens: A Mythology of Self* (University of California Press, 1985)

James Longenbach, *Wallace Stevens: The Plain Sense of Things* (OUP, 1991)

Wallace Stevens, *Collected Poetry & Prose*, Frank Kermode and Joan Richardson, eds. (Library of America, 1997)

Letters of Wallace Stevens, Holly Stevens, ed. (University of California Press, 1996)

Helen Vendler, *Words Chosen Out of Desire* (Harvard University Press, 1986)

Poet Aware

DENNIS O'DRISCOLL ON A "PRODIGY OF POIGNANCY"

MARK HALLIDAY
Selfwolf
University of Chicago Press, £8.50
ISBN 0 226 31384 0

MARK HALLIDAY CUTS a very contemporary figure in his poetry – streetwise, wary of rhetoric, citing pop songs as holy writ. What you see on the front cover of his third collection, *Selfwolf*, is what you get: the poet as regular guy, his crumpled Levi's and two-tone trainers suggesting a cool and casual style, the telephone (he is photographed using a payphone) preparing us for a language that is intimate to the point of sometimes addressing the reader directly ("I was realizing that if I wanted to I could use the telephone instead of writing the poem", as Frank O'Hara – one of Halliday's influences – put it) but which is also rather prosy (wordiness and flatness are among the principal risks he runs).

Like Thom Gunn, the "sniff of the real" is what Halliday (born in Michigan in 1949) is after; he wants a poetry that is capable of evoking lost youth, of recording an average life, of giving expression to the consumerist cacophony of America with all its securities and insecurities. Since the fall of the Berlin Wall and the intermittent successes of the Ulster "peace process", questions concerning the relationship of poetry to oppression and violence have arisen with fresh urgency (*What was the connection between East European poetry and censorship? Were the Ulster poets a product of the violence?*). For all his laid-back air, Halliday makes a serious contribution to this debate, implying that poetry must be tested against inexperience as well as experience; that art cannot live on extremity alone:

> Did he once survive tornado,
> earthquake, flood? Absolutely not. And he sure as
> hell
> never crouched in a fucking jungle ditch while
> fucking
> AK-47 bullets sprayed mud on his fucking helmet.
> How does he think he can talk about fear?
> He was never tortured by the police of Paraguay
> or even arrested in Turkey. He has never spent a
> single night in jail ...

Up-to-the-minute though his poems are, Halliday keeps faith with old-fashioned ideals of truth and beauty. As someone who confessed (in the course of his published dialogues – 200 pages of them – with his former teacher, Allen Grossman) to "ignorance of trees, bushes, rocks, birds, and rivers and what they do all day", his notion of beauty is predominately human – female and young, preferably – with some inbuilt self-chastisement in deference to the feminist age. His pacy first collection, *Little Star* (1987), presents male lust in all its nakedness, however disapprovingly it may be regarded: "I wonder if any intelligent feminists / will ever read this poem. / I hope so; though the prospect makes me tense. / I wonder how much I have damned myself". In *Selfwolf*, he remembers his poem about a woman with "long bare legs":

> Embarrassed now
> I imagine a female editor
> who received 'The Woman across the Shaft'
> as a submission to her magazine – the distaste she felt
> – perhaps disgust she felt – I imagine her
> grimacing slightly as she considers writing "Pathetic"
> on the rejection slip...

For Halliday, poetry is the ultimate preservative. To find words equal to the challenge of documenting and perpetuating ordinary experience continues to be the task he sets himself. He frequently draws on his memory bank and one is struck by the elegiac air which can attach even to his more celebratory moments. He was a prodigy of poignancy, feeling the pain of lost youth when that youth was in its full Sixties swing: "Richard played both sides of *The Early Beatles* at least twice, / and we all got the point: the point was that at twenty / we could already be nostalgic for vanished youth". Halliday has written poems which – to paraphrase Alfred Corn – will make his readers nostalgic for the American youth they never had: the student dorms, the hitchhiking and foreign travel, the night drives at speed to the beat of a Derek & the Dominos album. *Little Star* was a book with a pulsing soundtrack ('Bell Bottom Blues', 'Key to the Highway', 'Hello Goodbye'); though the volume has been lowered, music still vibrates through some of the later poems also. And if Halliday's soundtracks are cinematic, so too are the tracking shots which they accompany. Someone steps "out of Sax's Steak Sandwiches / with a large Coke to go, / straw stuck thru plastic lid". A paperboy walks "a forgettable side street back of the hardware store / down from the brick Methodist church". A layered reality is Halliday's speciality: a snatch of song, a chance remark, a recollection, an observation occur spontaneously and simultaneously; his poems reach for understanding through evocation.

Halliday's memories – of little significance in themselves – are elevated above banality and triviality by pathos, a pathos derived from his overpowering sense of evanescence. If "nothing gold can stay", what hope for the less gilded moment when "A truck bearing the name of a potato chip company / makes an assertive turn and clunks out of sight in the rain"? Whereas, in *Tasker Street* (1992), Halliday had agonised over "loss loss loss of what we feel and think", memory overload is the problem in the more recent 'Removal Service Request', a poem in which his possessions have tales to tell that are not of the bedtime kind:

> It is 2:45 A.M. I can't sleep. The apartment is too
> noisy.
> It's totally quiet. It's filled with the noise of the past.
> How does anyone sleep after the age of thirty-five?
> Things
> gather in your apartment and stay, each thing learns
> to emit its own signal, its own night-noise...

'Removal Service Request' is a good poem which falters towards the end. It is followed by 'Tonette', a poem which lurches from weak start to abysmal finish, Halliday's prose mimicking poetry not unlike the way he describes having mimicked a musical performance at school. His poems can be risky edifices – daring, sprawling, tentative, improvised – and they require the strong cement of his speech rhythms to stave off collapse.

Alan Bennett has wryly commented that "Cars abandoned by the road nowadays often bear a notice saying 'Police Aware'. Maybe one could slap 'Poet Aware' on a beauty spot or even on some particularly touching vagrant". Mark Halliday's awareness level is extremely high; and, instead of settling for poetic clichés of the landscape or bleeding heart variety, his books offer a widescreen vision on the richly representative experiences which he captures with comic yet rueful brilliance. His own ironic self-awareness is part of the picture, because the doubts, dilemmas and delusions that surface in his work are themselves so characteristically contemporary. True to the rituals and mores of its time, *Selfwolf* is a *Beowulf* for an unheroic age:

> Last night when I washed the dishes every move I
> made
> had a heroic kind of distinction. Do these two forks
> at once,
> rinse them swiftly, drop them in the drainer deftly
> producing that satisfactory clatter, now do the plates,
> washing the bottoms as well as the tops, my left hand
> so acrobatic in its connubial cooperation with my
> right –
> where is Martin Scorsese, doesn't he want to get this
> on film?

TWO POEMS BY MARK HALLIDAY
EL VIVO AZUCAR

See the man seated in the coffee shop
where a Spanish song of yearning plays.
Or is it Portuguese? That's not the point.
The song is full of brashly simple violins
and Iberian syllables of cultivated yearning.
This coffee shop could be in Santiago or Barcelona
or Rio or a suburb of Philadelphia that's not the point
the point is this sad man. Look how handsome he is!

Isn't he? Wait, look from this angle,
lest his nose seem too sharp. He sits very still.
He is knowing

that the world is about compromise
and that refusing this takes impossible energy.
His coffee is strong and good. And yes, also sweet.
He has made several compromises this weekend
but detail on this is not the point
O amigo corazon manzanas viento labios mujer hacienda
por favor and now
he is at one with the Spanish song in its meaning
that graceful acceptance of cruel disappointment is
our only reliable beauty. Coffee shops are good for this.

Now, this particular man could never build a house
with a grand redwood veranda and stone fireplace
and winding staircase, never, but let's pretend he could –
because then his stillness in the coffee shop,
at one with the Spanish song, is more sad and impressive,
because he seems to have realized
that merely physical structures will never satisfy the soul
(though coffee shops should be maintained)
and realizing this between sips he is so handsome.
Caramba! We love him!

SEVEN BASKETS

And then I sprang from the silver taxi
onto the vermilion carpet in front of a certain fine hotel,
a hotel tall and confident with windows buttressed in gold
like the aura that buttressed my casually athletic gestures
though this was in fact the hotel where in a previous life
I suffered a certain humiliation amid a committee
and/or when a woman embarrassed for me shook her head
and changed the subject – but now that past was to be
redeemed with such comic fullness I had to chuckle
striding through the great glass doors and nodding
very slightly to young dressy people who recognized me
and murmured behind magazines about my importance.
I was now a necessary part of something very large
without which humanity would seem a petty mechanical thing

and I flowed along the lobby on the steady wave
of being indispensable. Then from an elevator stepped

Deirdre who had seemed to ignore me last year
but now with a new blonde streak in her hair
rather obviously indicating her need for approval
she saw me suddenly and stopped and her cheeks went pink
and I knew, I knew I had only to propose a drink
and in less than two hours, in just seventy-five minutes
we'd be in the huge bed of my room Room 507
with Deirdre making little sounds of almost desperate hunger.
And this was all clear of any moral clouding
because I was not now married despite what was true
in my other life, that life all stuffed and bricked
with memories and the shrinkage of recriminations.
So then for hours at least five hours the eager breasts
of Deirdre served as a cinematic focus around which
the zest of my being constellated itself while
everything I did was music, my every motion sang itself
like the Dell-Vikings when they sang 'Whispering Bells'
and Deirdre was lit up like a peach entering God's mouth
because she knew she could never get luckier than this!
I felt sweetly sorry for her amid the cascading pleasure
because I sensed that in the morning she would neatly vanish
into some gray traffic of transmission trouble and fiancé
while I washed my hair and then in the gold-appointed cafe

I drank the hotel's superb coffee and said "Mallarmé"
at precisely the moment needful to silence several critics
and then roaming humorously I arrived at a gleaming gym
for an intense three-on-three game which I caused my team to win
by making seven baskets in a row. Seven!
Including two hook-shots and a reverse layup. Yes.
And then by a process tedious to explain in words
yet strangely lubricated and offhand

the basketball victory led to a party in someone's mansion
where both rangy Teresa and confectionary Connie
used dancing as a way to compete for my attention.
On the breezy moonlit balcony I knew sublimity was available
in several forms but sex was the most convenient;
Teresa and Connie both seemed hypnotized by my big shoulders
and my candid gaze which set a new standard

for self-assurance in the history of athletic poets.
With hilarious swift panache between rooms upstairs
I gave thrills almost frighteningly sheer
to Teresa and Connie in turn, not failing
to reap full unambivalent recompense, and then
I strolled back to the moonlit balcony and wrote
a poem so rich it made normal living look like sawdust
and then I published it in ten prestigious journals
and just acted gently modest when people said it was great.

TWO POEMS BY KAREN VOLKMAN

The rain falls on the empty town and "The rain falls on the empty town". There are no facts, just cages cross-hatched on a page. If my words for you were skeletal, quiescent, not flat wrecked runes but luminous bones, what animals would grow from these vestigial mazings? If it roars, it's hungry, feed it. If it bleats, cut its heart out, eat it. If it bleed...

Not that they're lambs or lions, no simple twinnings. No tusk no tooth no tongue says am enough, or sing to the reverend keeper her grim flaying. A species of three-winged flutter, or pearly paw. Pewter pelt, raw rigging, jarred jawing. Fang and fin.

You lose the world and win a gamey zoo; but won is less than least when I lose you.

MAY

In May's gaud gown and ruby reckoning
the old saw wind repeats a colder thing.

Says, you are the bluest body I ever seen.
Says, dance that skeletal startle the way I might.

Radius, ulna, a catalogue of flex.
What do you think you're grabbing

with those grey hands? What do you think
you're hunting, cat-mouth creeling

in the mouseless dawn? Pink as meat
in the butcher's tender grip, white as

the opal of a thigh you smut the lie on.
In May's red ruse and smattered ravishings

you one, you two, you three your cruder schemes,
you blanch black lurk and blood the pallid bone

and hum scald need where the body says I am
and the rose sighs Touch me, I am dying

in the pleatpetal purring of mouthweathered May.

Elliptical Stylists

by Roddy Lumsden

STEPHEN BURT

Popular Music
CLP / Colorado, $29.95
ISBN 0 87081 555 5

BRIAN HENRY

Astronaut
Arc Publications, £7.95
ISBN 1 90007 233 5

IN ALAN BOLD'S biography of Hugh MacDiarmid, there is a picture of a meeting between the great Scot and Robert Lowell. MacDiarmid is an old man, Lowell is only a few years away from his somewhat poetic death, clutching a wrapped portrait of himself in the back of a New York taxi. Nowadays, poets don't have to wait till their dotage to communicate with their cousins from far-flung parts: we find the world is politely closing in on itself, with cheap, fast travel, international publishing, the web which is world wide, reading exchanges and the dispersal of narrow national literary traditions which used to link poets lug to lug, like jigsaw pieces. So I shouldn't be surprised then to open these books by two American poets (both younger even than a Johnny-come-lately such as myself) and find that Brian Henry has a poem about my home town of St Andrews (as well as a version of one of my own poems!) and that Stephen Burt has another singing the praises of a two fine Scottish popsongs by my namesake Roddy Frame.

It is important to note that both Henry and Burt are deeply involved in the business of poetry: Henry became editor of the acclaimed international magazine *Verse* in 1995 at the young age of 23 and has edited a forthcoming anthology of younger US poets; Burt is a graduate student at Yale, with a particular interest in Randall Jarrell, and is already a critic of sufficient stature to have appeared alongside Marjorie Perloff and Helen Vendler at a recent conference in New York City. Both, too, have links to England: Henry's collection is published in the International Poets Series from the Lancashire press Arc, while Burt regularly reviews for several UK journals and was featured in Carcanet's *New Poetries 2*, edited by long-term supporter, Michael Schmidt.

The other evident connection between Burt and Henry is their lack of a dominant register, their eagerness to shift between styles, between the traditional and the post-modern (a word of which neither, I fear, will wholly approve). This is not to be mistaken for the try-outs and workshop pieces which sometimes fill out first books – it is clear that these poets have squared with their influences and decided that moving in several directions at once is the only sure way to move ahead. Such changing of gears, though approved for elder statesmen such as Edwin Morgan and Peter Redgrove, is largely frowned upon in the work of younger British poets, and it should be said that key debuts by recent British poets – Don Paterson's *Nil Nil*, Alice Oswald's *The Thing in the Gap Stone Stile*, Paul Farley's *The Boy From the Chemist's...*, Kate Clanchy's *Slattern* – have all benefited from a strong, singular voice.

Henry's most noticeable tic is a love of setting off at a gallop into long sentences – 'Veterans' Club' kicks off with a sentence of nearly sixty words and follows that with another of ninety or so! Yet the poem has plenty of linear stagger and swoony music to help bring it off. In other poems, though, I found myself confused by Henry's stylistic pulsing, as in 'Shelter':

> rust gathers its fellows into ranks of behave,
> weeds wrench through pinion and the rack
> words stretch themselves across as cries
> roost in the shelter of scree, on command.

Central to the collection is a sequence of twelve subtly linked pieces, 'Bystander', which begins by invoking a boon: "To test the silence because it's there to be entered... To skew the portrait so carefully centred" then sets out on a nautical journey which visits Scotland, Florida, Melbourne and Ireland, complete with another Henry tic, the use of proclamatory first lines ("The river holds down the mud holding up the river". "The summer holds the day to its word". "The silence of the banyans blinds".).

As with many poets who shift styles, Henry is perhaps at his best when he creates a hybrid, as in the short sequence 'Gravity', where unusual imagery and symbolism is married with a plaintive tone (the plaintive being a recurring note in Henry's work, and very well handled), "horseshoe crabs and stingrays hold // sand between their teeth / and grin / or seem to / in such light that brings / the human to every empty thing". He also has his eye and ear tuned for chaos: one couldn't imagine Henry staying long in a mudslide area, or in a house the morning after a debauched party, without pulling out his pad to make some notes for a poem. In 'Jasmine Tea', we find "the woman asleep / on the flea-hopping carpet, golden / Mingo licking her cheek". and in 'The Investigator...', a less fortunate moggy: "I found the cat in the toilet, / clawless, eyes looking nowhere // but downpipe". Henry can also be funny – see the eccentric travelogue of 'Roam' – and the book ends with a long poem, 'What They Remember', detailing the bizarre, contradictory statements made about one man's life and times.

Stephen Burt is another shape-shifter (he has stated that "no good poet is entirely typical of anything") and one can trace mini-lineages to the generation before him – an Ashbery line ('Arriving Clouds') and one to the reflective, philosophical school which is now somewhat dominant (the collection has been both blurbed up and awarded The Colorado Prize by Jorie Graham). Yet if Burt, like so many young American poets, has been tempted by post-modern strands, there are signs he is less sure now – at the recent conference (his essay can be found in Issue 11 of the excellent *Jacket* website journal- www.jacket.zip.com.au), he spoke of how dull, confessional poetry in the 1980s had lead to the spread of difficult and experimental poetries. However, "now it's disturbing to see how readily computer programs can simulate the farthest-out, least-referential, innovative writing".

It's interesting to read a of list the features which Burt notes in much contemporary US poetry – "ellipsis; apparent semantic incoherence; uncertainty about who or what is speaking; very busy verbal surfaces; repetition, in preference to rhyme...": most of which are still turn-offs for the majority of UK and Irish readers and writers. There are aspects of all of these features in Burt's collection, *Popular Music*, but that would give the wrong impression about what is better and simply described as one of the most impressive and enjoyable collections I have read in recent years. At heart, Burt is, I would suggest, traditional, lyrical, even Romantic, but this is popular music played at times on unfamiliar instruments and all the more catchy for that.

There are poems about writers, several based on works of art and some fine versions of poems by the Spanish poet Jaime Gil de Biedma, but the best work here is where Burt gives us more of himself, reflecting and weighing up, as in 'Inventory', a valedictory piece at the end of a season of summer school: "...rapid-fire / emoluments of names, half-empty boards / whose black, scoured flatness no spotlight can pierce". In the short, opening poem, 'Kudzu', he recalls a climbing plant which overran a porch, then twists the poem perfectly in the direction of another childhood memory.

But Burt's master-stroke is an exquisite love poem, 'A Sudden Rain in the Green Mountains', towards the end of the book. In long sentences which Henry would be proud of, it slithers past you, slightly obtuse, on first reading, then hooks you on second or third reading and holds your attention for as many readings as you care to take:

> Out here I can believe
> That all companionships only rehearse
> or faintly copy ours, and make it plain –
> As over the plain inn, the plain roof clears –
> That granite, marble, nascent evening stars
> And that impressive dinner bell, the moon,
>
> Still seem – may seem, to me, forever – yours...

Both these books come as ambassadors of a new generation of young American poets; both are challenging and highly recommended. What they have over many of their UK counterparts is a willingness to experiment and a wider diversity of immediate positive and negative influences. The downside is that I would be hard pressed to say "that is a Burt / Henry poem", shown one blind, in the way I could tell a Paul Farley or a Kathleen Jamie. Both poets have a fair amount of work available on the web, which I would urge you to have a look at, as a taster which I hope will send you to a bookshop or website to buy these books. As for me, I hope to meet them both soon.

The Anaesthete

by Rod Mengham

BILLY COLLINS

Taking Off Emily Dickinson's Clothes
Picador £6.99
ISBN 0 330 37650 0

"NON ANGLI SED Angeli" Pope Gregory I is supposed to have exclaimed on encountering British slaves in the market-place at Rome. Billy Collins's typesetter takes the opposite view, desacralizing his poems by converting the title of his second book *Questions About Angels* into the more utilitarian *Questions About Angles*. This typo is the second in the book, one of three that occur in the biographical note and the colophon well before you get to the serious stuff. The other mistakes are over the date of Collins's first book and the title of his third, elsewhere known as *The Art of Drowning* but here given as *The Art of Drowing*. "Drow" is an obscure Scottish word meaning drizzle. Maybe the errant typesetter has a point.

The minor (minor?) misprints are utterly in keeping with the mild misprisions that typify the sort of conceptual ploy every poem is built around. Collins selects an angle on everyday American life that is strange, but only slightly strange, and then just keeps the engine running, puttering along with a monotonous whimsicality and an unrelentingly middlebrow form of panache. In the end, this is about as defamiliarizing as a slightly animated J. Crew catalogue. One of the poems is actually woven around the contemplation of a mail order catalogue: 'Victoria's Secret'. It is the longest poem in the book, yet despite its pedantic itemising of hooks and eyes, straps and seams, it shows no insight into the culture of desire, or of arousal, or of sexual curiosity, any more than the title poem, 'Taking Off Emily Dickinson's Clothes', with its disconcertingly aimless frisson. More disconcerting still is the barrage of plaudits that greets the reader of the cover of this book. John Updike, E. Annie Proulx and Carol Ann Duffy all vie for first place in the Billy Collins Fan Club, while Michael Donaghy is on record as saying, "I'd follow this man's mind anywhere". Well, so would I, except that I can't find it anywhere.

The anonymous blurb-writer ups the stakes by declaring that Collins is a writer "of immense grace and humanity" who "shows how the great forces of history and nature converge on the tiniest details of our lives". This is precisely what does not happen in Collins's work. Humanity is kept at some distance, subjected to the deactivating rhythms of a prosing narrative voice that appraises every kind of experience with the same rueful self-satisfaction that comes from mastering the genre of the school report. The themes of many of these poems are suitable for exercises in a creative writing class. They comprise a series of generic statements in the first person which refer to ideas of history without ever engaging in the movement, texture or tone of history. Their reports on the progress of American cultural and social life have no real immediacy, no force of gravity, no colour; they are exactly like verse-equivalents of a scene from *Pleasantville*. This is a poet who actually blunts the variations of pitch, accent, stress. Billy Collins: cosmetic surgeon of the voice.

Most of the fantasies in the book are well-behaved, perhaps especially the ones about taking off other people's clothes. Interestingly, they become slightly more lurid when they contemplate cleanness. 'Purity' is one of a small group of poems about writing which equates the act of composition with stripping down to essentials. Collins likes to imagine himself taking off his own flesh as if it were a suit of clothes, precisely because it is contaminating and burdensome. Anything more than skull and bones consists of "flounces", as if the carnal were supplied by Victoria's Secret. The flesh is alien to Collins and to his work, which is practically allergic to passion and lyric intensity. The poem 'Advice to Writers' insists on sterility as the precondition for the writing of poetry:

> Even if it keeps you up all night
> wash down the walls and scrub the floor
> of your study before composing a syllable.
> Clean the place as if the Pope were on his way.
> Spotlessness is the niece of inspiration.

The Pope is nothing if not a big dirt-kisser, but that does not distract Collins from his sanitising, antibiotic mission. Poem after after poem inhabits a germ-free environment which is decently arranged before the subject is put to sleep. Paradoxically, a poem about the euthanasia of cats which thinks it is protesting at the extinction of individuality provides a formula for the reception of Collins's work: '"Painless" he reassures me, "like counting / backwards from a hundred". This is a countdown to nervelessness: verse-taxidermy. Billy Collins is a writer of immense piffle who only shows us how to make poetry smoothly negligent of history's impact on the details of our lives.

SUSAN WICKS
SCRATCH

I shall live out my life in soft cotton,
my flaking skin innocent
of the spaced red welts of buttons.

In the narrow mornings
I'll lie hardly breathing
on glass, watching the street turn milky.

Towards lunchtime I shall possibly
put on my quilted gown, its silk tassels
dangling, slithery as fishes.

I will keep watch on my hands,
muffle my fingers' itch in summer gloves.
Nothing will touch me

but a slick of unguents
in labelled jars delivered to my door.
At the prescribed hour

my good husband will anoint me,
turn from me in a rasp of blanket,
his mouth falling open.

All night I'll scratch
while blood sings in my broken skin
like salt, until death comes to me.

Museme

by Karen Volkman

LARISA SZPORLUK
Isolato
University of Iowa, ISBN 0 87745 704 2

CHRISTINE HUME
Musca Domestica
Beacon Press, $15
ISBN 0 8070 6859 4

LEE ANN BROWN
Polyverse
Sun & Moon Press, $11.95
ISBN 1 557132 90 9

IF THE FLURRY of anthologies of younger American poets appearing in the U.S. this year has revealed nothing conclusive regarding the Younger Generation, they have served to point up the very healthy state of poetry by women. Some of the most exciting recent debuts have been by women actively engaged in fashioning a tough and complex idiom in this reputedly post-feminist age. Not the least gift of the 90s has been a new mode for addressing the sensual; the appearance in 1995 of both Anne Carson's *Plainwater* and Lucie Brock-Broido's *The Master Letters* introduced an erotics of erudition, a rare fusing of intelligence and ardor, and helped give rise to the diverse poetic freedoms of the three books I discuss here.

Isolato, Larisa Spzorluk's second book, follows her 1997 debut *Dark Sky Question*. Like that book, the new collection is a series of short, meditative lyrics, assuming deceptively conventional forms – neat stanzas or narrow blocks, and clean, spare lines. But Szporluk's intensely unsettling vision quickly becomes evident. The first poem begins "inside the body" and the poems proceed in faithful adherence to hiddenness and an intense, inner listening, registering every intrusion from the outside with the shock of violation. Szporluk's imagination is engaged most deeply with the elemental, and her exploration of the world's violent incursions on the self focus on plant, animal, water, air – other forms of existence in all their inhuman workings. Her definition of world is misalliance – fisherman and fish, bird and stone, inside and outside, God and heart, man and wife – and every contact is dangerous, if not deadly. One response is refusal, the rejection by the nascent of its instinctive imperative to growth: "In the not-yet-world, not-yet-mouths / are saying no, // no to color, no to a molecular / engagement to each other, // no to the infant / water's plan for webless hands, // hands that grab at once, ten digits / clamoring for land. ('Realm of the Fern').

Both style and vision owe much to Louise Gluck's austerity and Sylvia Plath's severity. Poems of splintered family life and sexual violation are more disturbing for the absence of narrative pathos; fused into the book's imaginitive texture, they register with the integrity of obsession, in painful, dreamlike shreds.

Christine Hume's *Musca Domestica* is a book of equally shrewd, feinting strategies, though extending from a different tradition. Taking its title from the Latin for housefly, Hume makes of this everyday shameless gleaner (and survivor) a metaphor for the poet's work, the perceiving mind's digestion of trash and scatter, and (almost certainly) the traditional women's role of transforming the domestic. Where *Isolato* finds strength in resistance and stasis, Hume's poems take movement as necessity – "I am a blind engine climbing. I am essaying – my aid is error". In its best moments, this openness to accident combines with a formidable intelligence and rigor to produce a knotty, intricate, fascinating design. "To lie is to initiate a world, a traveling", and the erring mind's misperceptions or deliberate misrepresentations create a range of unstable landscapes, from the bitter comedy of 'Various Readings of an Illegible Postcard' to the false definitions of 'Report' and 'Total Things Known About Motion' ("movement is an ancestry"). Though the impulse to motion may be "blind" and instinctive, it is most often sight, that transgressor of distances, which brings the mis-interpretable world to mind: "shadows skim the skin debris: mumbling her into shape: say her brain needles when she looks into the edge: lake of dumb and numberless sight: the lucid parts only reflect: still saying how to keep herself overheard: I could show you myself were I near you" ('Lies Concerning Speed').

Hume adopts a range of prosodic frames to give shape to this roaming, and her management of craft is one of the book's great pleasures. She ends her final poem acknowledging her alter ego's ruthless, meticulous grazing: "Even flies come to the eyeball for food".

In contrast to Szporluk and Hume's stubborn solitudes, Lee Ann Brown sees poetry as a social, public interaction – a party to which everyone is invited, including cats and children (Brown teaches poetry in the New York City public schools through Teachers & Writers Collaborative). The voluminous pages of *Polyverse* encompass love poems, word games, puzzles, lists, notes, grafitti, found poems, and collaborations with fellow poets. Brown claims the lineage of Gertrude Stein, using wordroots and sound association to spin out into play. "A wild thing with language is what I deserve", and the wildness peaks in the section 'museme' in which each poem's title letters provide the unit for variation, as in 'Noon Eons': "Yo, Mom, Mnemosyne/nee Nosy Synonym./Yes?/No?" Elsewhere, the freefall gives rise to stories from a myth-tinged South: "Dora Dunlap Woolfolk Draper – / She liked elkmeat best. Stitched silk / over her hymn book approved by the Holy Fathers". The whole book rides on the noisy current of a city life full of voices and bodies, meetings and collisions, appetite and impulse: "Even as we speak I might be writing / an acrostic with your name. / What's the use / in cutting up? What about explosives? / I glow among poets. / Dress up for it. Unspeakable" ('Coffee').

In her spontaneity, generosity, and unabashed eros she is also a clear heir of Frank O'Hara, whom she invokes in 'To Jennifer M': "...Old-fashioned emotion / is relegated to a loud radio / void sometimes, but Frank O'Hara / has faith in you & me even / though or because we're girls".

It's this faith that makes each of these books so compellingly rich. And a corresponding love and pressure set toward language itself – as all three of these word-beholden women know, "Grammar lessons its fits and starts".

TWO POEMS BY DAVID BERMAN
WORLD: SERIES

When something passes in the dark
I make a note on a pad kept by the window.

Candlelight wobbles on the walls,
over the baseboard electrical outlets
that look like primitive swine masks

and I can't remember if I read or dreamed about them –
a sect on the Mayflower called the Strangers –
four or five adults who gathered in the hold
and spoke to no one through the three month passage.

When the boats landed on the beach
they walked into the North American forest
and were never seen again.

I put my book down and come to the window
where curtains are fastened to the sides
so it is like looking out at the world
through the back of a teenage girl's head

and my signature is drawn in magic marker
on the lower right hand corner of the window

So when something passes in the dark
it's captured for a moment inside my work.

I come to the window and title the eras
Monday, Tuesday, Wednesday,

and watch the wind in the tension of the blown trees,
the moon illuminated by my attention.
When something passes in the dark,
I try to tell its side of the story.

"I am passing someone in the dark", it thinks . . .

THE CHARM OF 5.30

It's too nice a day to read a novel set in England.

We're within inches of the perfect distance from the sun,
the sky is blueberries and cream,
and the wind is as warm as air from a tire.
Even the headstones in the graveyard
      seem to stand up and say "Hello! My name is..."

It's enough to be sitting here on my porch,
thinking about Kermit Roosevelt,
following the course of an ant,
or walking out into the yard with a cordless phone
      to find out she is going to be there tonight.

On a day like today, what looks like bad news in the distance
turns out to be something on my contact, carports and white
courtesy phones are spontaneously reappreciated
      and random "okay"s ring through the backyards.

This morning I discovered the red tints in cola
      when I held a glass of it up to the light
and found an expensive flashlight in the pocket of a winter coat
      I was packing away for summer.

It all reminds me of that moment when you take off your sunglasses
after a long drive and realize it's earlier

and lighter out than you had accounted for.

You know what I'm talking about,

and that's the kind of fellowship that's taking place in town, out in
the public spaces. You won't overhear anyone using the words
"dramaturgy" or "state inspection" today. We're too busy getting along.

It occurs to me that the laws are in the regions and the regions are
in the laws, and it feels good to say this, something that I'm almost
sure is true, outside under the sun.

Then to say it again, around friends, in the resonant voice of a
nineteenth-century senator, just for a lark.

There's a shy looking fellow on the courthouse steps, holding up a
placard that says "But, I kinda liked Reagan". His head turns slowly
as a beautiful girl walks by, holding a refrigerated bottle up against
her flushed cheek.

She smiles at me and I allow myself to imagine her walking into
town to buy lotion at a brick pharmacy.
When she gets home she'll apply it with great lingering care before
moving into her parlor to play 78 records and drink gin-and-tonics
beside her homemade altar to James Madison.

In a town of this size, it's certainly possible that I'll be invited over
one night.

In fact I'll bet you something.

Somewhere in the future I am remembering today. I'll bet you
I'm remembering how I walked into the park at five thirty,
my favorite time of day, and how I found two cold pitchers
of just poured beer, sitting there on the bench.

I am remembering how my friend Chip showed up
with a catcher's mask hanging from his belt and how I said

great to see you, sit down, have a beer, how are you,
and how he turned to me with the sunset reflecting off his contacts
and said, wonderful, how are you.

TWO POEMS BY JOHN STAMMERS

HOUSE ON THE BEACH

The shadows mediated by the slats of the venetian blind
stripe the silk finish ceiling;
I am reminded of the sheen on the ocean
of glossy magazine horoscopes I so deprecate,
am I not, after all, a logical and serious-minded Virgo?
Apparently, Venus is poorly aspected in Pisces
or something. I am practically nodding off at this point.

I expire across the bed with its sails full of disquietude,
its balsa-wood hull dipping and rising
on queasy unconsciousness like some *Kon-Tiki*
out to prove to me, as if I needed it,
that I am not new,
that I cannot get away from it all,
that *it* is *all* there is, and that my slumberings
retain the tell-tale signs of you
with your female body
and mouth full of explanations.
I fetch up onto this morning,
so strangely bright with exotic birds and fruit
but still with its hoard of old stone heads.

But just how did it get here, this place –
in the margins of buying and selling
or from somewhere in the veneered wardrobe
between sharp suits or materials
pre-weathered in the cutting room?
My new denim jacket had sand in its pockets,
that's how they distress them, you told me,
perhaps that's what the sand has done to me.
I am in distress, I had said, in body language
by rubbing the back of my neck; I am sand-blasted!

Or did it float up amongst all the debris?
It could have bobbed in at the cusp of beach and sea,
replete with the tactfully blanched flooring
and these hard little shells
that virtually stab your feet to death,
but that would be so hackneyed,

surely a place like this would be more original.

And another thing, who was it that said
don't build your house on sand?
Some old deity I think.
But rocks erode away into sand
and, like Thales said,

isn't everything just water anyway?
And he should know, having fallen down a well
trying to read the future in the stars.
And when everything is liquefied and clean,
wouldn't he be pleased, the old prognosticator,
if he himself hadn't already melted?

I strain to hear your breathing in almost the wash
of the water's edge and the lisping of the shingles
as they deliquesce into the sea;
I am asphyxiated with desire
to stroke the fine hairs of your body
and, as the sea runs over driftwood on the beach,
follow the subtle undulations of you.
I am filled up like an inflated tear
whose surface tension is so taut
that one more image of you with your poise –
your bare arms, your hands lightly crossed in front of you –
and I will break and shower into droplets like the waves
as they smash into the old wooden tide-breakers
and annihilate themselves in the air.

STELLA

You wanted to live in a geodesic dome
by Buckminster Fuller. Through the skylight's fractive lenses
of our polyhedral home,
we could spectate on the very axes
of the universe, you said,
the blue entropy
of the heavens falling away from us as we lay
like two androids in the white spaceship of our bed,
the local star-chart developing in the darkroom
of the firmament – Polaris and Proxima no nearer, in fact,

to each other than I am,
now, to you or the constellations
that rain down cancers on our heads
in their serio-emissions –
all that live amidst all that dead.

Once, before physics recalled you into the black,
you whirled round the white-carpet lounge
in a freeform fandango,
your ghost thrown up by the tablelight's orange
glow, your long hair, your dippy farrago,
your bare feet tiptoeing a Pentangle
track, the woollen fingers of the carpet
intimate between your toes, the skirl
of your silken dress in a widening flirt
as you spin, spin, spin and spin –
and what does the world do but spin?
I watched you till all the clocks went bong,
the spring stopped and everything
wound down forever.

Out here tonight, the pulsars click their half-lives
in the interstices of my blinks – so much time I never
saw out there, just the insides
of my own eyelids. I waiver
on the decking of our world inside a sphere and trace
the points of Cassiopeia.
I am like Rutger Hauer at the end of *Blade Runner*;
the rain pursues and outruns itself down my face.

THE REVIEW PAGES

Mannerly Ferocity

DAVID WHEATLEY ON A POET STILL ON THE WAY UP

JAMIE McKENDRICK
Sky Nails: Poems 1979 – 1997
Faber, £8.99
ISBN 0 571 20178 4

THERE ISN'T MUCH to link Matthew Arnold and Jamie McKendrick, but two things they do have in common are volcanoes and mermaids. In 1852 Arnold published 'Empedocles on Etna', a dramatic poem about a Greek philosopher who hangs around a volcanic crater. Vowing that he is "not to be all enslaved" like other men, he exultantly jumps in. Though McKendrick is still with us, the title of his second collection, *The Kiosk on the Brink*, commemorates a visit to another such summit, indulging his passion for these "burning conduits threading land and ocean / from Iceland to Patagonia". The marble fly that gives its name to McKendrick's last OUP collection has been "perfectly preserved" on a Roman wall relief, "much stiller than life and harder": "It can't have been long after / that much the same idea / occurred to Vesuvius". Athanasius Kircher emulates Empedocles in 'The Vulcanologist', which McKendrick has shaped like a volcano, by exploring the inside of Mount Etna, though unlike the Greek he wisely stays attached to a rope. As McKendrick writes in a translation from Montale, "The earth's rind is finer, more close-grained / than an apple's skin"; in another poem he proves the point by taking part in a seismographical survey.

Quakes and lava aren't the only threat to the usual lines of demarcation between the earth and other elements in these poems, which is where the mermaids come in. In Arnold's 'The Forsaken Merman', a woman refuses to elope with her fishy friend. In McKendrick's 'Mermaid' it is the man who tries to keep the mermaid on land, having fashioned her in a kiln, until a sea-storm washes her away, leaving only "a silt of potter's clay" in the boot of the car where he's been keeping her. The man in 'Il Capitano' unsuccessfully attempts the same escape.

Strongly defined surfaces are very important to McKendrick then: he likes rough textures and edges, mountainsides, scaffolds and stucco, but always with the opt-out clause of a seascape nearby, Mediterranean for preference. A primary influence here is Montale, as he announces by putting a customs post and a cuttlefish shell in *Sky Nail*'s first two poems, recalling two classic Montale titles, *Ossi di seppia* and *La casa dei doganieri*. Rarely have puffs of wind been as charged with Ligurian mystery as in McKendrick, though a passage like this from 'Ill Wind' is almost translatorese, down to the peculiarly delayed "the whole Sahara" in the sixth line:

> To talk of the weather was a morbid sign.
> The winds blew wherever they wanted to
> raining their freight of dust.
> A week before, the sirocco had come
> with its tiny pouches of sand, transplanting
> one grain at a time the whole Sahara;

McKendrick is one of a number of contemporary poets (Eiléan Ní Chuilleanáin, Peter Robinson and Harry Clifton are others) who have turned Italy into a privileged elsewhere. For early McKendrick though "the importance of elsewhere" mostly outweighs the need for any counterbalancing "here". *The Sirocco Room* contains a sequence on 'Lost Cities', which, you half suspect, is the way he likes them. In the words of 'Decadence', they are an adventure "that made no sense to me, but sense / was not what I was after". There's a poem here dedicated to Michael Hofmann, and McKendrick shares Hofmann's relish for affectless cool, accessorised with all the right bric-a-brac, one-star hotel backdrops, and stations where trains stop "for practice I supposed". Also like Hofmann is the take-it-or-leave-it quality of poems about an obviously difficult relationship, like 'Nostalgia' and 'Axle-Tree'. He's fond of striking a languidly mannerly pose when writing about something ferocious – especially when writing about something ferocious in fact, as in 'Ye Who Enter In', a version of the

Spanish poet Machado (was it McKendrick who gave Don Paterson the idea for *The Eyes*?):

> To write as a chisel writes on rock
> so every phrase you write resounds forever:
> ABANDON ALL HOPE ... You first.
> No really I insist please after you.

But cheerfulness keeps breaking through, in his recent work at least. The opening poem of *The Marble Fly*, 'Baleful Auguries', begins with the phrase "The year began with baleful auguries": by the end of the poem we've got no further than "Next year began with baleful auguries". This coy delight in understatement, lingering on the threshold of what it wants to tell us, is familiar McKendrick; what makes the rest of the book so refreshing by contrast is the poet's new willingness to go beyond archness and lightly ironised detachment, two whole books of which was frankly more than enough. After so much earth, fire and water the numerous poems about birds, insects and other flying contraptions in *The Marble Fly* give notice that McKendrick is taking wing. Emotionally, too there's a new freedom, and it shows. The tender 'On/Off', about a pair of earrings, ends with the image of a burden thrown off:

> Then the lobe's set free
> and breathes with delight
> to shed the slight weight
> of the earrings.
> Earrings that might be
> twin filaments, a pair of ball-bearings
> or a hammock-faced moon and a tarnished star.

But McKendrick doesn't have to reach for the stars to achieve poetic take-off. There's a poem about the modest delights of bicycle transport, but better again is 'A Roman Ruin', a tribute to a clapped-out old banger going nowhere fast. The telescoped social history, skilfully resisted sentimentality and McKendrick's monkeying about with cliché and scraps of quotation (the rolling stone, the rejoinder to Du Bellay's "*Nouveau venu, qui churches Rome en Rome*") combine to make it a small contemporary classic:

> RIP Wolseley 1500, MOT
> failure cum laude, rust-plaqued, cough-racked jade,
> eyesore, ossiary, tin tub, dustbin
> – that last oil can was your extreme unction.
>
> What's left can be my memento mori
> or a monument to Britain's now decayed
> industrial base. There's a sepia postcard
> bluetacked to your walnut dashboard
>
> of the ruined palace of one Septimus
> – weeds feasting off its arches much as moss
> (some rolling stone) does on your window rim.
>
> *O pilgrim, you who search for Rome in Rome...*
> Forget it. Neither the Tiber nor the Thames
> will be graced again by your ancient chrome.

Sky Nails is a fortuitous sort of book, given that its main reason for existing is McKendrick's change of publisher (is three books enough for a *Selected*?). But if the motivation for *Sky Nails* isn't as true as it should be, it's at least *ben trovato*, as the proverb has it in his beloved Italian. This isn't a survey of a talent that's settled down enough for us to know what to expect next, even to the extent of knowing if he can build on his strengths rather than lapse back into mannerism. Let me take a bet on his future then and suggest that, like those airborne machines in *The Marble Fly*, he's still on the way up.

Nature Morte
by Caitriona O'Reilly

THOMAS LYNCH

Still Life in Milford
Cape, £8.00
ISBN 0 224 05159 8

THOMAS LYNCH IS one of an elite and enviable band of writers who possess a steady income. Whether diplomatic duties influenced the modernist expansiveness of George Seferis or St. John Perse, what impact insurance assessment might have had on the composition of 'Thirteen Ways of Looking at a Blackbird', or the link between Dennis O'Driscoll's dark drollery and his life as a civil servant is anyone's guess. But the memorable opening of Thomas Lynch's 1997 collection of essays, *The Undertaking*, is a reminder of why he must have been a godsend to his literary publicist: "Every year I bury a couple hundred of my townspeople. Another two or three dozen I take to the crematory to be burned. I sell caskets, burial vaults, and urns for the ashes. I have a sideline in headstones and monuments. I do flowers on commission". An undertaker who is also a poet and essayist must surely possesses a singular wisdom on matters mortal as well as promising to satisfy some of our less commendable prying instincts. Rather like the comedian Ali G, Lynch's first books *Skating With Heather Grace* and *Grimalkin and Other Poems* had a distinct novelty value. But there are only so many times Ali G can ask "is it because I is black?" before the joke begins to wear thin, and in *Still Life in Milford*, alas, Thomas Lynch falls victim to the same malaise. A poem like 'Couplets' ("Two girls found dead. My sons go to the morgue. / Two cots, thick rubber gloves, two body bags") illustrates why dramatic subject matter alone does not guarantee a successful poem. The poem comprises a structural and linguistic repetition of twos, but is overburdened by the extreme self-consciousness of Lynch's craft. Yes, we know that he is of Frost's opinion that words can provide an essential stay against horrors and confusion (and he has seen more horrors that most) but in this short poem the repetitious lulling and formal straight-jacketing lead to triteness: "Too long stuffed in a culvert, raped and stabbed, / too decomposed to recognise. Too sad". There is an excessive reliance on our awareness of his unusual profession, and not a thorough enough exploration of his subject: "Today the wakes and paperwork details. / Tomorrow a burning and a burial".

This tendency is everywhere in evidence. Lynch's obsession with statistics, with "doing the math" as he puts it (exhorting us, with Muldoonian brio, to "go figure"), indicate the tension in his work between a reliance on the spurious authority of broad generalization and an ethical recognition of the particular. In *Still Life in Milford* the former tendency wins out. One of Lynch's more familiar tics is a random listing of the paraphernalia of contemporary life, a habit he has indulged so frequently in his prose that it has by now lost much of its effectiveness. It is there in the otherwise witty and skilful title poem of this collection too:

I have steady work, a circle of friends
and lunch on Thursdays with the Rotary.
I have a wife, unspeakably beautiful,
a daughter and three sons, a cat, a car

good credit, taxes, and mortgage payments
and certain duties here. Notably,
when folks get horizontal, breathless, still:
life in Milford ends. They call. I send a car.

We are so familiar with this technique that our response is ever more likely to be "so what?"

The so-what effect is induced, similarly, by an over-reliance on rhetoric, which follows generalization as inevitably as *rigor mortis* follows expiry. One poem is actually entitled 'A Rhetoric Upon Brother Michael's Rhetoric Upon the Window' and the homespun-philosophical questions of which it is composed ("What if the window is for looking in – / where we abide with our personal saviours / who save us from ourselves? Are they gods enough?") demonstrate an overwrought Romanticism of questionable authenticity. I suspect the dangerous influences of Yeats and Heaney in Lynch's reliance on rhetorical constructions and the "singing line". But Lynch lacks the precision of his precursors, as his frequent repetitions indicate. His misuse of the word "noisome" ("Is it in their silence that the noisome / truth is spoken, the body's hunger hushed") is a case in point. This word recurs with monotonous regularity in both his prose and poetry, where it is apparently intended to mean clamorous instead of noxious – a solecism which should have been editorially nipped in the bud. Elsewhere, "son" is almost always preceded by the epithet "darling" and there are far too many references to "the heart".

Argyle the sin-eater, Lynch's cohort in the mortuary business (who owes something to Heaney's Sweeney) makes a reappearance here too, but the Argyle poems are generally some of Lynch's strongest, as though he finds the use of an alter ego liberating. And lest we forget that Lynch has more than one string to his bow, many of the poems in *Still Life in Milford* are set around his ancestral home of Moveen in West Clare – although occasionally Lynch's lapses into Clare dialect teeter perilously on the brink of "oul' sod" tweeness: "And after Sinon died, 'twas Nora sold / eggs and new potatoes till the debt was paid...". Elsewhere, Lynch puts his obsession with lists to most effective use in a poem which mimics a pathology report and is entitled 'One of Jack's'. Kevorkian I presume. Aidan Mathews successfully used this technique in 'At the Nurse's Station' from his last collection, but Lynch's controlled, deliberately detached narrative goes one better. Its impact is devastating. A wry, slangy, streetwise humanity enlivens Lynch's best prose and poetry – and in this I'd include the horrifyingly tactless curse poem from *Grimalkin* which, so a recent essay tells us, the author lived to regret. "A poet writing against his genius will be like a prophet without his afflatus," it has been said, and Lynch is at his best when he is being tough on himself, not when he his straining towards the transcendental ether. But maybe his constant references to "frequent flier miles" have something to do with this. Or perhaps he is confusing being a poet with being a prophet, which is a curious mistake for an undertaker to make. Either way, *Still Life in Milford* could have done without the afflatus.

The Vinyl Seduction

by Sarah Wardle

RODDY LUMSDEN
The Book of Love
Bloodaxe, £7.95
ISBN 1 85224 509 3

IN 'AMERICAN PIE' Don McLean asked "Did you write the book of love?" Now Lumsden has written it. Seductive fantasies and anecdotes about sexual antics lie alongside mysterious pieces and deeper poems to his partner. He moves deftly from the modern 'Incident in a Filing Cupboard' to 'Always', a timeless fantasy about a farmer's daughter. He shifts easily from the laddish speech of 'An Older Woman' – "she said the world revolved around her. / I know exactly what to do without her" – to an aesthete's tone in 'Piquant': "which, when I lean in to take the kiss, / says *fool for sugar*, says *mammals one and all,* / *says never again a love like this*". He is as skilled at portraying a drunk at the bar in 'Tricks for the Barmaid' – "See? / It's only a matter of time before she sleeps with me" – as he is at depicting a medieval French alchemist in 'The Boyhood of Fulcanelli'. He is as good at the metre of conversational patter as he is at the rhythms of lyric. Lumsden is particularly effective at combining traditional poetic forms with his wit. 'Lithium', for example, subverts the sonnet form with content about casual sex rather than love. Elsewhere traditional subject matter is rendered contemporary. In 'Athena' he juxtaposes classical art with kitsch, imagining that Athene created the Eighties posters of "the New Man, Michelangeline, in black and white, / whose new-born son is mewing on his sculpted chest", and "that blonde who lifts her tennis skirt up to display / one perfect buttock".

Wit is a weapon of seduction and there is plenty here. There is humour, as in 'Against Naturism', written in praise of clothes, which "must be better than a foreskin snagged / on gorse thorns or a cold, fat nipple jammed / in the scissor drawer", and in 'Troilism', which depicts "Y who, with an erection in either hand, / said she felt like she was skiing". There is Wildean wit, evident in the aphorism and word-play of 'Subject Matter: History': "Well, let's be honest, / ... go down in history and not down on it". But there is also wit in the sense of sustained conceits. 'The Beginning of the End' brilliantly sustains the sci-fi idea of a man with special powers, whose "*Fairy Liquid* bottle" contains "anti-chaos" and in whose airing cupboard police find "the nine tenths of the iceberg which usually lie / below the water / which I'd been saving for a rainy day". 'In the Wedding Museum' adapts the Miss Havisham image of decayed marriage items and effectively sustains the museum conceit. Though Lumsden excels at wit, he can also be serious, whether about love, as in 'Response' – "But if they made your madness better, / I'd follow north the winter weather: / one less horror in your cast of terror" – or rejection, as in 'Show and Tell', where a shamed schoolchild stands with "pearl tears on the red puff of my cheeks; / their laughter booming down the blue hall, / shaking the little coats on their pegs".

Some of the poems read like fables enabling us to foresee how our own affairs might conclude. In 'Marmalade' one of the zesty lovers pauses midaction to guess how things will turn out:

So, toss a coin on which will happen next

from all the oldest stories in The Book
of Love: sweet zeros, trains will rattle by,
a husband's car will pull into the drive,

we'll turn out to be twins or some such thing;
she'll pair my socks, she'll sigh, she'll wear my ring,

then leave me at the end of Chapter Five.

Here 'The Book of Love' is seen as a bible full of parables from which we may choose our own story. The closing poem, 'Lullaby', is an example of Lumsden's gentler, lyric voice, where his affection spans the alphabet from "A to L, my love, and M to Z". It suggests the trace of a different reading, in which we might see the collection as an address book we can use to make a date with each poem.

Lumsden's hip wit and laddish patter may suggest a comparison with Armitage, but he has recently written: "I deny suggestions that Simon Armitage has been a major influence on my work". Perhaps the similarities, the modernity, the half-rhymes and the metrical momentum building to memorable conclusions, are merely coincidences to be blamed on the *Zeitgeist*. Lumsden has his own voice, his own obsessions. Moreover, other echoes may be detected, such as that of Douglas Dunn in 'Glasgow', 'Edinburgh' and 'Class'. In 'Pagan' MacDiarmid appears as a hero. Song lyrics are also an important influence. Perhaps they represent a common ancestor for both Lumsden and Armitage and the whole Lit. Pop scene. In *The Message* Lumsden explored the crossover between poetry and pop. He borrowed from the Beatles for the title of his first collection, *Yeah, Yeah, Yeah*, and plundered pop again for this one. The twelve hands photographed on the cover conjure up a class reunion and suggest that the book speaks to the *Friends* generation, with whom it is likely to be a hit. In *The Message* Lumsden compared a PBS Choice to going "straight in at Number One". *The Book of Love* should stay at the top for many weeks. It could even become a classic.

A House of Books

by Ian McMillan

JIM BURNS
Beats, Bohemians and Intellectuals
Trent Books, £7.99
ISBN 0 905 488 57 1

I ONCE WENT to Jim Burns's house to interview him for a radio programme I was making about British Beat poets. I've never seen so many books in one house in my life: it was as though I'd stumbled into an art installation called House of Books. At one point I had to go upstairs and there was just a narrow passage of stair carpet between the piles of books at each side. Maybe some people don't know who Jim Burns is: he's a poet, editor (of *Move* and *Palantir*, two fantastically influential and important magazines of the last three decades), and perhaps most importantly, a reviewer and essayist, chronicling the margins of literature; the forgotten poets, the outside influences, the one-novel novelists, the figures who clambered to edge of the public eye for a brief second and then fell off the edge. This collection of essays brings together work from the mid-sixties to the late nineties, and it's like a tour of Burns's house, a wander up his stairs, and it reminds us how small and narrow the accepted literary canon can be.

There are writers in here that, thanks to the efforts of people like Burns, are now well known, like Charles Bukowski, but there are also writers in here who really needed rescuing, like Lew Welch, a poet who figures in Jack Kerouac's books as Dave Wain, but about whom I confess I knew very little until I read this book. His poetry has a beat sensibility, a deification of the ordinary, as in these couple of lines about driving a taxi; "When I drive cab, / I watch for stragglers in the urban order of things. // When I drive cab / I end the only lit and wakeful things in miles of / darkened houses". Welch was an interesting bohemian who in the end simply disappeared. As Burns writes "But if he did commit suicide his body was never found. And if he simply disappeared to the Southwest, as he said, then he has managed to stay out of sight ever since".

Staying out of sight is something that's happened, by accident or design, to a lot of the writers in this book: who now remembers Kenneth Fearing, novelist and poet who tried to celebrate a proletarian language and setting, as in poems like 'St. Agnes' Eve': "The settings include a fly-specked Monday evening, / A cigar store with stagnant windows, / Two crooked streets; / The characters: six policemen and Louie Glatz. / Subways rumble and mutter a remote portent / As Louie Glatz holds up the cigar store and backs out with $14.92"? Who can quote the poems of John Montgomery, or

Lenore Kandel, or David Raphael Wang? Jim Burns could, and he wants us to be able to, alongside our rich diet of Bloodaxe, Faber and Carcanet poets.

The book ranges from Burns's early exposure to American culture as a young man in Lancashire and later in the Army, via explorations of important little magazines like *Satis* and *Migrant*, to essays on individual writers like the ones mentioned above and including Seymour Krim, Robert McAlmon, Kenneth Patchen, John Montgomery and many others. What really excites me are the wide open spaces opened up by these pages, and the opportunities they offer for diving into these lost works and swimming around to the heart's content. Burns reminds me of the importance of underground publications, of bohemian scenes and long nights in flats with books up the stairs talking about books and words and poets, and it reminds me that so many writers have been forgotten and so many are out there (in second-hand bookshops, at car-boot sales, at jumble sales) just waiting to be found, like friends at a party you didn't know you were invited to. I'd love to see a *Collected Jim Burns*, with all his essays and reviews in one volume, but until that comes out I'll be satisfied with this. It'll look good on the stairs.

Nightlife and Morality

by Stephen Burt

Thom Gunn in Conversation with James Campbell
Between the Lines, £10
ISBN 1 90329 100 3

BETWEEN THE LINES publishes book-length interviews with well-known poets. Previous subjects include Anthony Hecht and Michael Hamburger; Heaney, Muldoon, and Richard Wilbur are (it says here) on the way. This volume gives us an informative, friendly 42-page Q&A between Gunn and critic, biographer, and *TLS* eminence James Campbell, conducted in January 1999, after Gunn had completed what's now his new book, *Boss Cupid*.

42 pages isn't "book-length" is it?

Not really, but there's a very extensive 42-page bibliography attached – it cites every uncollected poem, essay, and interview; translations into Czech and Italian; and book reviews and critical studies, including pages devoted to Gunn in books on other topics. And there's a new poem, 'Clean Clothes: a soldier's song':

How else then could I stay
Adequate day by day
  Drenching each crease,
Without the thought of change into
  Dry clean clothes that renew
The anonymity which holds me in one piece?

Here, dryly and elegantly (as usual), the poet admires both an unruly guy, and the impersonal systems of discipline in which that guy finds his strength.

Gunn's new book, Boss Cupid, *is catching attention for poems in the voice of Jeffrey Dahmer, Milwaukee's famous cannibal-serial murderer. Does Campbell go there?*

He does. Gunn says that when he read them aloud, and some older listeners rose to leave, he exclaimed: "Ladies, I'm very sorry to have upset you, but Jeffrey Dahmer didn't kill nearly so many people as Napoleon or Julius Caesar, and you wouldn't have minded if I'd written poems about either of them, would you?"

Anything else on Boss Cupid?

Gunn's mother killed herself when he was "about fifteen". *Boss Cupid* has two new short poems, good ones, the first Gunn has written about that event. He tells Campbell the secret of writing those poems was to cast them in the third person: "Then it came easy, because it was no longer about myself. I don't like dramatizing myself". But it disturbs me to see the mother poems and the Dahmer poems treated as the book's foci. At the moment my own favorite parts of *Boss Cupid* – the ones that seem freshest – are the short, short-lined free-verse poems in the section called 'Gossip'. And the other poems about *characters* – the man "Raised, he said, not at home but in a Home"; the fierce but distant onetime lover whose "true / Passion" turned out to be maths, "cyphered in chalk beyond my reach".

Gunn has given several long interviews: there was a great one, with questions by Clive Wilmer, in a 1995 Paris Review, and there's another with Jim Powell in Gunn's prose book Shelf Life (1989). What does this one add?

Except for their brief chat about the new work, not much. To be sure, though, the key points of Gunn's life are hard to skip: it shouldn't surprise us that interviewers tend to ask him the same questions, nor that so careful a writer tends to give similar answers. We have Gunn's London childhood, and his mother's death. Cambridge, where "I met and fell in love with the guy I still live with", where "everything good happened to me". The Movement: Larkin "was a wonderful poet, but a bad influence". The difficulties of being a gay man in the Fifties. Gunn's California mentors of sorts, the doctrinaire poet-critic Yvor Winters and the mystical, charismatic Robert Duncan. Syllabics, which Gunn used well in the Sixties. Free verse, which "has to contain rhythms as interesting as those in metrical verse". The Sixties in San Francisco, and "acid – which we did an awful lot of". Gay liberation. Ginsberg. Donald Davie. Isherwood. Privacy. AIDS.

Anything else you liked?

Sure. I liked Gunn's comments about adolescence – he wants to downplay the differences between his and ours: "Everybody has an unhappy adolescence, don't they?" 'A Sketch of the Great Dejection' – that strange almost-visionary poem in The Man with Night Sweats, describes, Gunn says, "Not *sickness* and recuperation; *adolescence* and recuperation". And as usual, Gunn comes across as admirable: reserved about his private life, thoughtful about his principles. He's someone who's quite devoted to nightlife, to sex of course, to *fun*, and yet he's articulated a liveable moral stringency, and an entirely appealing way of connecting art to ethical choice: "You compare a book to a person, for example, or to an action". It's dangerous to take anyone's life as exemplary – that must be one of the differences between people and poems – but Gunn's in some ways can seem so.

Sticks and Spikes

by John Greening

ELTON GLASER
Winter Amnesties
Southern Illinois University Press, $11.95
ISBN 0 8093 2305 2

THE COVER OF Elton Glaser's fourth collection shows "dry sticks under a wintry sun", and that line from Yeats came to mind reading these poems by an American writer little known in Britain. Born in "sluggish" New Orleans, he lives in Ohio, regarding this sometimes as a "conversion", but more often as a Fall. From the very opening of the book, with its epigraph, "Everything cold can teach", the sense of exile is potent: "First month, month I was born in / Far from this day / That stays stuck at zero...", a motif taken up fifty pages later (with a nod to fellow Southerner, T. S. Eliot) in 'Zero Summer':

In the ghost zone, in Ohio,
I wake one morning
To bolls of snow,
As if winter had stripped bare
The spiky hedges and bred them
To cotton. Beyond my breath
Spackling the cold window,
I find my first world
Come back secondhand
From the South...

Reading Glaser is like looking up through a complexity of boughs towards a clear bright sky. The lines are brittle: their spiked presiding spirits are Giacometti, the crucified Christ, crows in a locust tree, or the junkyard run by the poet's father: "Where we live, / Everything around us is in ruins, / Broken, gutted, and cut apart". This collection of sticks and spikes is arranged in three sections. The first is preoccupied with youthful memories – Catholicism, adolescence, school, family; the second with the natural world and the mythology of Eden; the third with life after forty and intimations of the deathbed. But that feeling for a Paradise Lost is what drives the book. 'First Earth' makes the fallen world a "bower of bindweed and spiked rose", where the names chosen for the animals have become insults and the context of all experience has become sexual: "Her tongue took him quick as a toad's: *toad*, / A brooding bag of leaps whose name came late to him, / And only after hearing unrelieved for days / Her sullen theories and complaints". The loss of Eden sounds here like the end of a marriage. But also there is a sense in 'Nothing of Ourselves' that Eden was a "stifling paradise". Heaven is in that bare sky beyond the tangle of sticks: "The glass glare of the pond, on a day / All clouds abandon, gives back / Nothing of ourselves". 'Late Returns in Eden' suggests that the forbidden tree is dangerous because it hasn't yet been named, as if that process were an act of provocation, like putting up a barbed-wire fence. The serpent does not come. It is his absence and the consequent boredom that provoke the Fall: "Why won't he come? All the soft afternoon, / They miss his wit, his hiss and dreamy promises..."

If there is a depopulated feel to this book, there is certainly plenty of wildlife. It is at once a fascination, an irritant and a threat. The serpent, of course, but also the neighbour's dog; even a domestic hen "pecks away at anyone" while it suffers the "bitter repetitions of the roost". The few humans here have animal masks: like the neighbour behind his dog, and the 'Bird Lady' in her three-page monologue; only the poet's father rises vividly from his nest of scrap iron.

The book's final section opens with a quotation from Mark Twain ("People ought to start dead, and then they would be honest so much earlier") and launches into a poem whose wit and music and emotional accuracy had the required Housman neck-bristling effect:

THIS IS YOUR

Engraved invitation to
The coming-out party of the dead,
In autumn when the moon
Rises over shock and husk,
On a lawn where headstones lean
In the pose of Easter Island.
Wear white:
Suits and gowns and cerements,
As though the air tolled with
Perpetual bells of snow...

Not all of the poetry is this good. Some of the effects are just a little too pleased with themselves. He succeeds least when he tries hardest, and the set pieces (like 'Deathbed Edition') veer too far towards a Merrillian rococo. The two voices of Glaser are neatly demonstrated in the over-wrought 'Eine Kleine Nachtmusik', which is printed opposite the plain sonnet 'A Little Daymusic'. But I suspect Elton Glaser's most popular poems will be those like 'Smoking' (as featured in *Scanning the Century*): "I like the cool and heft of it, dull metal on the palm, / And the click, the hiss, the spark fuming into flame...", where the sinful aestheticized decadence of the act is allowed to breathe to a musical accompaniment worthy of Gerald Moore.

JAMES TATE
THE PLUMBER

When the plumber arrived to fix the water-
heater he eyed me with considerable suspicion. I
told him how grateful I was that he had come
and he actually growled at me. I asked him if
I could get him something to drink and he said,
"I don't want your stinking water". I pointed
him to the basement door and he spat at me
saying. "What, do you think I'm an idiot?" Then
I heard pounding and cursing from the basement
for the next forty-five minutes. I considered
calling the police, but knew they wouldn't
believe me. I considered getting in my car and
just getting the hell out of there. As he came
up the steps I could hear him whimpering, actual-
ly sobbing. He opened the door and threw his
arms around me. "I can't fix it!" he said. "I'm
a terrible plumber! I held him in my arms and
we rocked back and forth with me gently patting
him on the back. A little while after he was
able to leave, his wife called to ask if he was
alright. I said that he was just fine and she
thanked me very sweetly.

CHIRPY THE RUFFIAN

We were on our way out to the beach
to visit some whales we had gotten to know
slightly when the car suddenly exploded.
Mercifully, we were spared, or some of us
were spared anyway. Bodo looked as sharp
as ever, like a smoky Egyptian cat eager
to be fed. Perhaps some terrorist had
gotten to us, God knows we have made our
fair share of enemies! We were the Sand People,
we ate sand. The wind blew right through
and we kept walking, kept falling down.

BRIAN JONES
A QUARTET FROM RY

"...he took first of all the stalest, the most predictable plot..."
        Geoffrey Wall: Introduction to Madame Bovary *(Penguin Classics)*

I
A classic one-horse town: a spine of high street
with a few petering-out offshoots
like inadequate ribs.
Down at the pelvis end, a covered market
and a church a little apart, with a porch
"well worth a visit", from which
carvings still crisply visioned
gaze out over fields that rise
to where balers park great tawny rondels
tremblingly poised
as if ready to slip on the slither of cut stalks
towards the town, and plunge, and bury it all.
Already, myriad tiny outriders
gold-dust the table over which I gaze
to scan the neck of a girl with loose-piled hair
(as she nuances the banter of two young men
who clearly ache for her)
for beads of Emma's sweat.

II
The novel, dropped here like a plague-rat,
infests with fiction:
a toyshop shimmers as Homais' pharmacy
and a bank hallucinates an inn's clatter.
The river glints towards adulterous meadows
and my hand nearly touches a hand
in a supermarket transaction.
What squirms beneath official pride
when to live here day by day is to enact
deceit, humiliation, lust, betrayal?
The smudged evasive Guide leaves you bewildered:
Was it here, the dreadful amputation?
Here, the night of shifty promises?
Here, the black trickle from the mouth?
As if (just as he knew we always do)
someone flinched as truth came into focus.

I I I

Have you seen an *oubliette*?
(Such a pretty Fragonard word!)
I have, and I'm still running from it.
Five stone steps angle down into the difference
between a garden (presenting ornate Spring,
supervised by a Duc de Berry castle)
and a rim of plunging void,
black slithered sides
purchaseless to scrabbling
down which the chosen one was lowered
(slowly, carefully, don't dislocate the shoulders)
to be released there, where now dim tourist light
reveals something like a stage seen from the gods,
with, at its centre,
dropping still deeper, a smaller hole
for corpse and excrement.
Here, at the west wall of the church,
just out of vision of those sharp-eyed saints,
that terror catches me again
as I scan the stone all cameras come here for:
the piled-up names pile-drive her down,
Couturier, Delamare, Emma Bovary,
the triple claims of father, husband, Flaubert,
lapping her, like caskets of lead darkness,
in the horror of being someone else's story.
(Which drives all Flauberts into pre-emptive strikes).

I V

In a hall built awkwardly against the market
(stumbled on as I pack up to leave)
frayed-edged mauve screens are stuck with images
– old newspapers, photos, gothic-scripted
Nazi decrees.
A face follows me from screen to screen,
a Resistance family, a family from Ry,
maquisards who one by one were caught,
tortured, shot.
The exhibition lasts a week,
I'm here in its last hours (a woman
stops her dismantling and sits to let me see).
Low down, in the corner of one screen,
a German officer swings back his boot

to kick the head of someone lying there.
Above him, from two trees,
two men lean out like gargoyles
issuing screams.
They are strung from branches, their shoulders hunch
in dislocation like baby wings.
Spine, ribs, sockets –
I flinch from the impossible agony of these
It's not until I look again
(that first glance saw my pain and blinded me
to everything but pain)
that I see specific complex mouths
screaming not with agony alone
but with outrage and derision.
Surely a Nazi took this photograph –
propaganda? – to send home to the folks?
a fetish for a lonely passion?
Like mine, his fictions fade
beside the camera's unrequiring vision:
strappadoed bodies, swung boot, waiting head,
(unique components of a local hell)
and, above it all, two throats stretched out
to gutter something only they can tell.

FRED D'AGUIAR
FAITH

Christy, you're gone from me. I press my palms
together without your clasped hands in between.
I rub back blood into my hands until warm
when it should be your hand in my one dream
that I rub the blood from and back into, no balm,
just our hands' oils, finger by finger, no cream,
down to the crinkly little bone that won't hold
still when I press and rub against the cold.

I clutch space, an ache. I press hard.
I bruise my own flesh and eat my own words.
Since you've been gone I'm beside myself sad.
I saw a sun bloom in a sky and spore
every colour of a rainbow and felt bad
because you weren't with me to see it grow.
Your absence makes a razor of that sunrise
dragged across my salt-swollen iris.

I turn my back on such mornings for you
as one would on some thing too strong to stomach
to be any good, too good to be true.
Then there are the dawns I don't see so much
as hear – voices sweet as morning dew,
but I'm too busy searching such and such
a face moving across this sunstruck country,
to mind the birds as the sun makes its entry.

I am stripped bare by the light, bare and
lonely, my bones wrung clean, the clean
bones ground to dust, scattered in the four winds;
four deserts and four lakes have opened between
you and me, the two of us at opposite ends
of a compass, poles apart like dusk and dawn,
dark and light, black and white. We share the night,
we share the day. I am black, you are white.

Why couldn't we be either one or the other?
Not both. Why fight two battles at once?
How can we be in two places and together?
But in this place at this time every ounce

of skin conspires against our love. Gather
Trade winds, let the sky fill its ample lungs,
peel off my skin. Leave just flesh and bones;
and me, raceless, like dew, trees and stones.

To slip this skin, shed it for something new,
that's no colour on earth or in the sky. Raceless
like light. And our love as lithe as a minnow
on a river and the river all the lighter for the bless
-ing of a moon. The streets washed clean by dew,
by light. The houses painted from pillar to post
the one colour of love, which is every colour
ever seen, every colour dreamed, but ours.

I scrub, fetch, sew, wash, iron,
put wet things out, take dry things off
clotheslines, measure my days by the wrung,
beaten light journeying across the floor
in stripes, bars, wondering if your mind runs
the same way, if you do the same chores,
if you push wonder from your face, like a lock
of hair absently put behind your ear but

it won't stay there, falling in your blue eyes
again. You're not with me. You're with someone.
Somebody to keep you warm, who says, "Yes",
when you call love, darling, petal, woman.
You've forgotton about me. I am less
each day I'm absent, less than my name.
Absence is a wind that fans love's fire
or kills love's candle flame forever.

I did not mean your people to despise
you for loving me. If I could rub off the black
and be like you, to be with you....I realise
that I can't. I am black from head to toe, back
and front, black gums, black cuticles, black eyes.
You thought me beautiful, black made you ache
for more black, so much black I turned you blue,
your white became black and I became you.

Christy, I am still your Faith. Remember.
Daily I see your face and say your name.

I hug my pillow and fool myself its straw
is your red hair and me keeping it warm
is you warming me, loving me raw,
and me hugging it no less than your arms
returning my embrace. My face in that pillow
keeps the cold at arms-length, bans sorrow.

Can you see me as I see you? Can space
stretched between us out the light by which
our love thrives? When you conjure my face
you draw blank, a landscape filched
of trees and nothing except distance,
the faint line of a horizon; a land pinched
bare and us not there. Our thoughts bereft
of space and time until no thoughts are left.

When I sing I mourn your absent love,
Christy. I pull my hair, I wring my hands.
I twirl the end of my skirt like a glove
round my fingers. I do not enter, I stand
in doorways, linger, when I should leave.
I hope you will walk in or out as planned.
But you're away and you stay gone, with just
the remembered smell of you to keep my trust.

The you and not you in my life, my days.
The me and no you, never able to shake off
damp and cold; in heat, my hooded eyes –
my blind to shut out the whole world of
you not here with me. I harden in ways
you – if you were around – wouldn't approve.
My skin thickens, I smell, I don't care,
I twist the knots in my matted hair.

My nails grow, curl, and turn back in
on themselves. When I walk into a door
frame or miss the last step on a landing,
there is a hurt, a swelling, a jolt, or
a small fracture that happens to something
bearing my name, but there's no one, no her
to whom Faith sticks, no body to blame,
not even a she to answer to that name.

A child cries out, Mother! What Mother?
Who mothers? Not me. I hear a baby. I think
Baby. I'm in its vicinity. But that cry for her
means nothing to me. If it is meant
for me I am barred from answering it. I hear
misery. But I have enough of my own, thanks.
Behold need! But how can I answer
when need is my middle name, I swear.

I walk from that baby until its mewl
is a small sound, miles away, a bald bird
in dirt below its nest, the lost jewel
of a stray calf someone's bound to have heard
and will attend soon – but not this fool,
not me. Cries drown in my throat, a sword
I swallow over and over awake or asleep,
that makes my skin goose up, crawl and peel.

Locked in the wall of that Quaker house
Christy sweet-talked me, "My skin was dead,
a cover for my flesh, a faded blouse
worn carelessly, my bone-bag and bone-bed.
But with you skin is a sensation doused
in oil and set ablaze, something to be read
with you as my instructor, my skin as text
in our skin school of gaze, touch and reflex".

Christy promised me a first-born daughter,
then a son followed by another girl
and boy. I replied between our laughter,
"Its alright for you to promise the world
when I'll have to carry and bear them after
your work is done". "And what wonderful work!"
He yelled, rolling onto me in the dark;
his legs prising my thighs further apart.

"Not you only, Faith, the two of us.
Whatever you do, I do; when you fall
pregnant we'll bear our children simultaneous-
ly". "Yes! Christy, let's turn with you still
in me". So we hugged, hooked legs, pooled trust,
turned, without him coming out at all.
Christy, love fused our bodies hip to hip,

arm in arm, lip to lip, nothing else could fit.
There was nothing between us but skin,
nothing could get between us, not even
a blade of that razor dark, nor the skimmed
silence in that hiding place our uneven
breathing turned sweet then sour as sin,
or independent thinking. It was heaven
on earth, our just dessert, our big bounty,
for finding love where love wasn't meant to be.

I licked Christy's tight tummy which trembled,
oscillated like mercury in a dish,
then shrank from my tongue. I bent my head,
kissed and in the middle of each kiss
lifted my lips a fraction off him and burbled,
There, there, be still for me during this
examination. And sure enough the tremour
melted; he begged me to keep up my murmur.

Who said anything about stopping? I tried
to stop but found I couldn't help myself.
Christy laid his hands on my head, sighed,
and his own head fell back and he lifted
his spine and I swung my hands behind
his waist; the moist small of his back shifted
from side to side. Again he urged me on.
As if I needed urging. I was too far gone.

As was he. The two of us slaving for the wages
of sin; consumed by touch that hungers
for more touch, that can never be assuaged.
The two of us and no one else under
the sun when we were together, our bodies
welded into one by the glue of our plunder
of sin. If that's the name you must plaster
on our love, go ahead slave and master.

This tapestry of knotted arms and limbs
cannot now be undone; two hearts strung as one
won't be unstrung. After a man climbs
high and sees beyond the horizon,
how can he settle for the flat line

presented to him as the limit when he comes
down? He views all borders as a gimmick.
He strikes out on his own to beat that limit.

Love's for displaying in life's gallery.
Love wants to show off its intricacy.
Love won't be cooped up and pilloried,
or hidden away where no one can see.
Love spreads wealth world-wide.
Love shares the secret of its alchemy.
Everybody glitters in love's clothes;
love turns us all from base metal to gold.

In this extract from Chapter 2 of *Bloodlines*, a verse novel to be published by Chatto in September, *Faith*, a black slave in late 19th-century America, is separated from her white lover Christy.

KATE CLANCHY
TWO MONTHS GONE

It makes us want to shut all doors,
turn off the news, the phone, light
after light, pull the stairs, like a ladder,
up behind us, until, underneath the covers,
the outside pressing in upon us,

we are the pair in the heart of the tale,
the woodsman who spared the unicorn,
the kitchen maid who hooked a witch
from the well and held its tail
through fourteen fearful incarnations,

and won, walked home from the woods
with a wish like a brimming glass of water,
and when the promised goblin came,
sang out, in a single rhymed conundrum,
the answer: all we ever wanted.

In the dark after the thunderclap, we wait
for the crooked town to wake, find
gilded rooves, loaves on each table,
for the crowds to come, half-dressed, incredulous,
for our fortune, squalling in its cradle.

JOE SHEERIN
MAKING DO

The bricklayer doesn't ask the brick
If it's comfortable there. If it lies snugly
Enough along the line and takes
The weight above it, it will do.

The roofer doesn't ask the tile if
It minds the weather. Cunning as survival
It casts the drop on the one below
Spreading the misery. The ground
Bulky and enough of it absorbs all.

The finished house doesn't ask the occupier
Who pays the bills or starts the arguments
Or whose turn it is to turn off the light.
It has learned its lesson and sits tight.

The spermatozoa doesn't ask the ovum who
Started the foreplay but gets down
To the business of geometric progression.
The finished baby lies like love on the carpet.

CAROLE SATYAMURTI
ELEGY

I
Dusk, and the boathouse keeper
calls the late, scattered boats,
from beyond the curve
in the lake; calls them by name,
Hirondelle, Euridice, George Sand.
Are they real or imagined,
those smudges of black
in the shade of the far bank?
Again the boathouse keeper calls,
his voice carrying, returning.

II
What's in a name? You are,
in the name I called you by,
Sathyaji; its weight and shape
hard to convey – except
it lent itself to tenderness,
teasing and respect; closeness
and a certain distance.
Now it's a vessel
for the far-flung,
only sure reality of you.

III
Love draws you back.
In saying it, I see your name,
boat-shaped and luminous,
prow stitching the dark,
returned from formless drift
about the world. Let me
gather up your shattered selves;
I've threads enough – a skein
of versions. I'll recall you
differently each time.

IV
Nothing can be held, or hurried.
Wind casts a shiver on the water;
shallows, uncertain
in the withdrawing light.
A phalarope races its image
and is gone; reflected, relinquished,
unreachable as the distant boats
the boathouse keeper calls and calls,
only a name to summon each of them.

Yet, here they come.

BILLY COLLINS
WINTER INVENTORY

I forget who called death
the man in the Chinese nightgown

but I do know Melville's dates
and I can find the five Sorrowful Mysteries
on the fingertips of one hand.

The name Mathias Grünewald rings a bell,
but it is a bell that hangs from the neck of a goat
who is grazing in a distant valley.

And I don't recall ever hearing
of Paula Modersohn-Becker
before someone at a party last night
dropped her name on my foot.

I know *chrism*, *gnomon*, and *nugatory*,
but I had to walk the length of the reading room
today to look up *testudinal* in a public dictionary.

I can list maybe eight apostles,
a handful of muses, and only a couple of Caesars.

Then again, I never wanted to be the one
in the big red armchair
who is busy rattling off the succession of Popes
or even the governors of Delaware.

I would rather wake up in the morning
thinking only of the weather,
walk out along the reservoir
beneath the swift clouds and feel
the wind blowing through the holes in my head.

And at night, I would be happy
to sit cross-legged
in front of a snapping, throaty fire

with nothing on my mind
but the yellow wavering flames,
in which, every now and again,
I swear I can see the man in the Chinese nightgown.

MONIZA ALVI
THE CHILD GODDESS

Let us suppose that we have given birth
to the Royal Kumari of Patan –

the child goddess who blesses
marriages, heals the sick,

and gazes just to the side of those
who've reached the dark star

of puberty. Our personal deity –
We are so proud!

She no longer pulls our hair.
She doesn't have tooth decay.

Perhaps she'll be seven years old forever.
Everyone stares at her vulnerable face

and proclaims she has the cheeks of a lion.
At times we despair that she is never

allowed to leave our home except
when we parade her through the streets.

The most powerful of all virgins,
she is only permitted one friend.

We dress her in glittering scarlet
and sit her on a scarlet chair.

She clutches the arms of this throne
as if she is about to stand up

and run outside and play.
But she is utterly still, utterly quiet.

One day, inevitably
she'll graze her knee, prick a finger,

lose a tooth – her goddess status

disappearing with her first drop of blood.

She'll become a little like a real child.
Our Kumari of Kathmandu,

of the suburbs, of wherever we are.

TWO POEMS BY AUGUST KLEINZAHLER
FAMILY ALBUM

Loneliness – huge, suddenly menacing
and no one is left here who knows me anymore:
the Little League coach,
his TV repair truck and stinking cigars
and Saul the Butcherman
and the broken arm that fell out of the apple tree
dead
dead or gone south to die warm

The little boy with mittens and dog
posing on the stoop –
he isn't me;
and the young couple in polo shirts, ready to pop
with their firstborn
four pages on in shortshorts and beatnik top
showing her figure off at 16 . . .
1955 is in an attic bookcase
spine cracked and pages falling out

Willow and plum tree
green pods from maple whirling down to the sidewalk . . .
Only the guy at the hot dog stand since when
maybe remembers me,
or at least looks twice

But the smushfaced bus from New York, dropping
them off at night along
these avenues of brick somber as the dead child
and crimes of old mayors
lets off no one I know, or want to

Warm grass and dragonflies –
O, my heart

SUNDAY NOCTURNE

Red pulse the big jet's lights
in descent
        The aerial
on the plumber's duplex shakes.

Along these palisades the crowded
grids subside.
        Tonight

even lawyers
and hoods
approach the foothills of revery.

No pizza slice for the wayfarer
at this hour.
        Get thee to an inn, sport.

And still more jets,
dipping.
    From Dakar,
Akron and Samoa.
        A gentleman

in Italian loafers
disembarks.
Tomorrow at 1 he will bring
profound good news
to a steak joint in Moonachie.

REVIEWS

Disconcerting Places

by Hugh Macpherson

CHARLES TOMLINSON
The Vineyard Above the Sea
Oxford Poets/Carcanet, £6.95
ISBN 1 90303 901 0

JAMES SUTHERLAND-SMITH
At the Skin Resort
Arc Publications, £6.95
ISBN 1 90007 223 8

ALAN JENKINS
The Drift
Chatto and Windus, £8.99
ISBN 0 7011 6921 4

MATTHEW SWEENEY
A Smell of Fish
Cape, £8.00
ISBN 0 224 06067 8

GYÖRGY PETRI
Eternal Monday
Bloodaxe, £7.95
ISBN 1 85224 504 2

READING, LET ALONE reviewing, a whole batch of poetry books is – or surely should be – a disconcerting experience. When one reacts fully to a poem, that voice alone is the guiding one for the duration. A series of other rival voices is not only a distraction, but calls into question the process of responding for a time to the one lone inner voice of another individual, briefly abandoning our own vision. It's demanding too, like the business – that I've never understood – of listening to highly emotional music as background noise while one browses in record shops. Some people whistle along cheerfully to the most harrowing symphony. At the end of even a snatch of the Shostakovitch 8th, I'm ready to collapse into a chair and be revived by a team of counsellors and a malt whisky. So too with art galleries, and poems. If these creations mean anything serious, then to react to them *en masse* is to be swamped with emotion.

In the end, though, the practicalities establish a balance, where one receives each separate voice as a temporary travelling companion, to whom one listens and reacts but without being overwhelmed. When one has travelled with someone through disconcerting places, one knows them in a special way. A relationship of a strangely intense but limited presence – widely recognised as curiously close and difficult, but afforded no formal status.

It's maybe because of this that so much poetry does report back from a wide range of new places, as well as showing us the familiar from other perspectives. The disproportionate number of writers who incorporate in their work a time away from their first environment can't all be due to Byron and Lawrence, or to a desire for sun and sierra. Your voice reverberates in a different way, to yourself and others, in a strange place.

Charles Tomlinson

Many of Charles Tomlinson's poems in T*he Vineyard Above the Sea* are about visits to other countries. He comes across as a learned guide, admirable and fascinating, yet occasionally infuriating – as he opens new ways of looking, but sometimes also burdens us with context or information we don't want. 'The Blossom' has a fine vision of a flower of foam glimpsed on a stream, unnecessarily framed in a knowing opening line ("I never told you how...") and ending with another unduly pointing finger: "this tribute of a flower absent as the poet says from all bouquets". 'A Festivity' convinces immediately with its precise opening metaphor "flight-lanes imprinted on the sky in crumbling chalk" but then follows with a frenzy of alternatives. You want to rip the constricting frame off the canvas in these places, and keep only the heart of the thing, in the kind of disagreement that makes fellow travellers end conversation for hours at a time. Shortly afterwards, though, you regret your irritation when you come to another poem where Tomlinson's angle of vision and, more importantly, his precise ear for the words to convey that, get things exactly right – his hawks and fig trees "where a wind is rising with tidal sounds through the leaves" in Trebiano, or his "frost-fur on every gate and fence" and the "ticking... of melted drops".

I found myself impervious to the more deliberately literary moments – reading Gerard Manley Hopkins aloud at Epidauros, imagining Herman

Melville on the Acropolis, talking to Robert Creeley in the desert, Frank O'Hara in New York. Most of this seems a kind of greeting to absent friends, sent to us the unknown readers by the wrong email button. But when he observes that "I like something lucid, surrounded by something mysterious" I recognise a destination I'm keen to get to, one which he reaches admirably on many occasions here, as in 'Shorelines' where he looks at "where the certainty of land begins" amid "the tidal trickeries of water". At the end of this collection, going separate ways for a time, I found I missed Tomlinson's company and would seek him out again for a journey in future books. I'm glad that Carcanet have included him in their rescued Oxford poets.

James Sutherland-Smith

James Sutherland-Smith's *At the Skin Resort* is a more edgy and vulnerable performance, but all the stronger for that. It contains some of the best poems I have read for some time, and it seems curious that this is the first full-length collection we have had in twenty years. Sutherland-Smith lives and works in Slovakia, and is alive to all the odd business – invigorating and frustrating at once – of existing in a culture and language that you know but which you were not born into. (He has translated, with others, a highly interesting anthology of Slovak poetry *Not Waiting for Miracles*.) He is precise, evocative, descriptive, and wryly puzzled and bemused in a way that lets us share many of these journeys into places that it's hard to make out clearly, through the maze of history, language and sheer fascinating otherness. Shared experiences only go part of the way towards true belonging:

> This kopka of cut grass
> Is as tall as me, raked up
> By your first cousin once removed.
>
> He's ancient though and talked to me,
> As they do here, of the war;
> The Russians and the Magyars
>
> Thirty kilometres off,
> Tens of thousands dead. Which war?

Sutherland-Smith is excellent at conjuring up the shifting moods of relationships, both the serious and, what is more difficult, the light-hearted ('Rainfall and Domestic Economy'). He also has a very deft touch for evoking place, and has the ability to let the exact detail of flowers and birds and weather combine with the less available but more powerful miasma of intangible atmosphere. His best is when all these evocations come together in a poem that finds the structure to let them resonate at their separate proper pitches.

> Up in the moist woods of my foreign soul
> Out of earshot of any farm dog's growl
> I haven't found either light or dark
> But mergings, green on green. Differences
> In this cooler blankness, a crooked cross
> Or double-headed eagle scratched in bark,
> The fans and bells of Solomon's Seal
> Or yellow star of Bethlehem in moss
> Have offered me no earthly help at all...

Though he doesn't overdo it, other languages are properly part of his interests and an additional means of getting to grips with things.

> I go out after the long drawn-out vowels
> Of a day's freezing gale. I am crusted
> With the absence of human consonants,
> Labial, plosive, fricative, which break
> The mineral groan of weather.

He is the local resident who has the requisite knowledge but, more importantly, has retained awareness of the satisfying strangeness not just of this place but of all the world. His poems convey knowledge of places and people, and the excitement that goes with that – he is a worthy mentor for any latter-day Patrick Leigh Fermors who might pass this way across Europe.

Alan Jenkins

With Alan Jenkin's *The Drift* we are in an entirely different kind of relationship with both writer and environment. *The Drift* is also immensely evocative of place – of London, the river, the Kentish coast, Brighton – but as part of a journey into the past in exploration of relationships, with family and childhood friends. In an ironic 'The Road Less Travelled' he writes "I've never scaled the heights of Macchu Pichu with a backpack or trekked through India... I never wrote 'I have walked the sands of Dar-es-Salaam'".

There is a poem headed 'Barcelona' but the lines here which make you feel you've travelled a long trajectory in company with the poet are those conveying a distant Britain of the 1950s and 60s.

It's a landscape that seems almost prepared in advance for being lost behind us, a curiously lugubrious yet immensely potent and unreachable version of ourselves and others. One that we perceive, too late, as deciding what we are today.

> The pale sun of late October
> warms the stuccoed crescents, red-brick lanes,
> shutters of Refreshment Rooms, boarded-up arcades
>
> and you remember how it was you found each other
> in this past-its-best, out of season seaside town:

It's a Britain that was not far removed from Dickens, had moved on as far as Graham Greene's Brighton, and the Thames described by Joyce Cary in *The Horse's Mouth*. It's damp, depressing, full of beer and rain and wet shingle beaches, yet the very accuracy of the evocation indicates how important that lost world is to these verses.

> You grew inseparable here
> among the smells of salt, wet rot, stale beer
> walking into wind and fine rain that would drown
> the words you threw away like twice-smoked stubs.

It's a world of fathers who haven't ever spoken about the war or settled from it, of Airfix model kits at one end of adolescence and Cream and Fleetwood Mac with 'Tales of Brave Ulysses' and 'Albatross' at the other. What comes of this is uncertain. In 'Inheritance': "This is my inheritance. It is plenty". In 'House-Clearing': "What's left is guilt" and in 'Chopsticks' we're left with the shared meal and "*Go on, finish up that last prawn.* But I can't".

In the end the real inheritance is the collection of memories and loyalties that create this collection in all its ferocity of sharp nostalgia. Something heart-felt is going on here, though it's hard to describe it in anything other than the terms of the poems themselves – an indication of how very successful Alan Jenkins has been in creating a remembered world that can't be approached in any other way. This is powerful stuff, and despite its gloom and depression one finds oneself coming back for more because of the sheer imaginative force of it. Its remembered Britain is as exotic a location as any that travel could bring.

Matthew Sweeney

Matthew Sweeney's *A Smell of Fish* left me feeling rather inadequate, the kind of travel companion who's actually longing for a rest day when the other person is already packing for a particularly exotic departure, that might take some time, or forever. Ruth Padel, emitting praise words at machine gun rate, describes him on the back of the book blurb as "a unique force for good in British poetry", and goes on to talk about "a parable for the human condition" – a phrase I have to admit I've always regarded with some suspicion: we've had enough of those over the years. But I found Sweeney very agreeable company, tremendously frenetic. Whenever I turned a page he was taking a great leap of imagination out of the window, leaving the words and myself breathless in pursuit of him. In 'The Tunnel' he jumps in with

> When they opened the manhole
> on the street outside our house
> I wanted to climb into it...

and already he's emerging out of it at the far side of Ireland as I'm still peering in the entrance, wondering if I can squeeze my mental embonpoint through the narrow gap. In 'Hooves' he begins

> The sound of galloping hooves woke me,
> then a high, lengthy whinny
> pulled me out of bed to the window...

And again, while I was checking if he was still somewhere on the poem's original premises, he'd "locked the door and got on the horse... clutching the horse's neck, as his hooves rang on the road to Aldeburgh".

Sometimes I'm entirely ready to join in the clearly expected applause; at other times there's a certain "so what?" atmosphere as the hoof beats fade out, and why Aldeburgh anyway? But I've heard Sweeney read 'The Tunnel' to an audience that was entirely won over and ready to venture with him down all available flights of fantasy. If you're ready for a gallop, then he's an immensely winning poet.

György Petri

Of all these prospective companions for an extended walk, however, it's the Hungarian poet György Petri and *Eternal Monday* that I would most want to join for a conversation afterwards in some Budapest cafe. He has a reputation as a rather grumpy political dissident poet, but it's not the impression that I receive at all, either from this book or the earlier translation *Night Song of the Personal Shadow*. True, he's very rude about politics, but they don't seem to me his main obsession. He's sufficiently unconcerned to note ironically, about the dissident theme, that "The epoch expired like a monstrous predator. My favourite toy's been snatched". He seems, rather, someone with a deep distrust of all easy illusions and untruths, and communist regime politics have been one of the most blatant and pervasive scams, that he could hardly avoid dealing with, in any account of what was around him.

> Right here, now, what isn't *is*.
> It's the heyday of responsible fools
> and responsible knaves. No! No! No!
> I can't be doing with this, I won't have it!

What a pleasure to be reading someone who is so totally scathing about supposedly worthy illusions, and whose eventual praise of experience can be relied upon, therefore, to have found something truly worth savouring at last. In this translation he reads at times like W. S Graham, with the same curmudgeonly conversational concern:

> Forgive me for having troubled you.
> (As if anyone'd care
> a jot for such scruples over there ...)
> But of those left here so few
> phoning up would find me
> so irritable-anxious for their hello:

But having dealt with these things, he can conclude:

> Now only there is nothing but the *now only:*
> my wife, and what I think, and what I write.
> And come to think of it, that's quite a lot.

And he is both moving and convincing in 'Morning Coffee'

> I like the cold rooms of autumn, sitting
> early in the morning at an open window,
> or on the roof, dressing-gown drawn close,
> the valley and the morning coffee glowing –
> this cooling, that warming.
> The tide
> of day comes rolling in –
> in waves, gigantic, patient, barrelling.
>
> I can start to carry on.

Clive Wilmer and George Gömöri, the translators here, earlier gave us a volume of the poems of another Hungarian, Miklós Radnoti, which it would be good to see again. Another justification for ending in Budapest is that Hungary has produced such an unreasonably high proportion of, not just good, but really *fine* poets – Radnoti, Sándor Weöres, and, above all perhaps, János Pilinszky. Petri, in this book, seems to me one of their number.

Natural

by Ruth Padel

ELAINE FEINSTEIN
Gold
Carcanet, £6.95
ISBN 1 85754 449 8

MANY INFLUENCES HAVE gone into Elaine Feinstein's fine-wire lyrics. Feinstein is, surprisingly, a Liverpool poet (born there, raised in Leicester). In the Sixties she developed East European connections, both personal and poetic, and was a conduit into British poetry from the American "Black Mountain" school. Plus she is one of Britain's few major Jewish poets. From her first book (1966) all these different cultural tones, especially that East European lyrical edge, got concentrated in that spare, wry, musical, compassionate voice. *Gold* shows how, thirty-four years since her first collection, her poetry goes on growing, alongside her other writing life of novels and biographies. (Her *Ted Hughes* – he was a friend, an early patron of her work – is out next year.)

The book is in two halves. The first is 'Gold', an ambitious new departure which gives full play in her poetry, for the first time, to Feinstein's narrative skills (see the novels), and fascination with the material and/or emotional unfolding of an individual life (see the biographies). It is the eighteen-page autobiography, in five-line stanzas, of Mozart's librettist Da Ponte. As a child he wants to escape the ghetto and feels "only poetry could work the magic / of changing me into a European". When his family converts – "Knowing so little of what I was to enter, / I thought Christendom must be Paradise" – he flings himself into Christian education, especially poetry, lives it up disgracefully in Venice, briefly becomes an alchemist (though makes no gold – that appears, though Feinstein never spells it out, in the libretti of *Don Giovanni* and *Cosi*), tangles with the Inquisition, get his teeth wrecked by a girlfriend's lover who feeds him nitric acid, works for Mozart, gets into terrible debt, emigrates, and winds up an American Professor of Italian Literature. It's a great story; the verse sweeps you along with lovely visual detail en route. But in its tumbling vision of eighteenth-century Venice and the Austrian imperial court, the poem is also a meditation on Jewish estrangement-from-within. Always entering new worlds "across the cusp of a new age"; always having to adapt, chameleon-wise, to Christian cultures to create its own new poetry or life.

The book's second half contains lyric poems, also about people: friends, family and historical characters like Abishag, the young girl tied in bed to an elderly king, to rejuvenate him: a lovely version of Rilke's poem. They are lyrics of emotional insight with a wonderful music of vowel and syllable. Internal rhymes follow each down the line. Take –

> the baytree left
> to my attention, withers on the window sill,
> and moths lay eggs in the lentils, while
> still hurt by memories of you as gentle, I'll
> look into a monitor for comfort…

At the centre of these lines is that "lentils"/ "gentle" relationship, ringed by two related rhymes, "while"/"I'll" and, outside that, "sill"/"still". Yet what you notice on first reading is not technique, but pain. Or follow the long I from "mind" to "kind" to "died", in her poem on the death of Ted Hughes. (They are a sub-genre already, Hughes' death poems, but hers is also about an old friend). The central stanza opens with a dream dreamed the night he died: "In my mind, he was standing in our old / Cambridge kitchen, his face like mountain stone, / his presence solemn and kind". It ends with the news in the morning: "he had died". Same long I, but without that softening N.

This poem's last verse leads towards the final syllable of a word which always features in discussion of Hughes's own work:

> We travelled through fields of mud
> towards North Tawton Church and funeral,
> seeing wet dogs and hovering birds
> as he had: all creatures of a brutal
> planet, to be observed with love, knowing
> their cruelties include the human animal.

The patterning of "funeral", "brutal", "animal", the way "love", not quite at the end of the line, echoes "mud" via the widened vowel of "hovering birds", gets that mix of cruelty and love in, and for, human and animal nature which is characteristic of Hughes's poems, and also evokes the title of Hughes' first book, *The Hawk in the Rain*. So while the poem is about grief for the man, it also embodies the way other people's poems have been enriched by his work. It is very clever; but not obtrusive or willed. The music simply makes it seem that silent next step beyond "animal" in her sound-sequence: natural.

METRE

**288 page
American Special Issue
guest-edited by Chris Agee**

A.R. Ammons,
Louise Glück, Jorie Graham,
Donald Justice, Robert Pinksy,
Charles Wright
and many more.

**Available for £8 from
David Wheatley,
Department of English,
University of Hull,
Hull HU6 7RX**

REVIEWS

Royal Festival Hall
Queen Elizabeth Hall
Purcell Room

October 6-14, 2000
Royal Festival Hall & Purcell Room, London SE1

Announcing...
Poetry International 2000

Fleur Adcock
Yehuda Amichai
Yves Bonnefoy
Kamau Brathwaite
Ciaran Carson
Hugo Claus
Billy Collins
Michael Donaghy
Carol Ann Duffy
UA Fanthorpe

James Fenton
Tua Forsström
Lorna Goodison
Lavinia Greenlaw
Marilyn Hacker
Kathleen Jamie
Jackie Kay
Liz Lochhead
Michael Longley
Christopher Logue

Roddy Lumsden
Claire Malroux
Jamie McKendrick
Edwin Morgan
Andrew Motion
Les Murray
Sharon Olds
Bernard O'Donoghue
Don Paterson
Dorothy Porter

Dimitri Prigov
Jo Shapcott
Penelope Shuttle
Matthew Sweeney
Dane Zajc

Readings, talks, workshops, filmed poetry, kids events and more.

Register NOW for your free programme:
email Literature&Talks@rfh.org.uk or call 020 7921 0971.

Supported by Royal Mail. Funded by THE ARTS COUNCIL OF ENGLAND. sbc

---

MA in Writing (part-time or full-time)
A writing course by writers for writers

This distinctive course with annual intakes in September and February is taught by practising writers and addresses both aesthetic and commercial concerns in writing (next intake September 2000).

In addition to a core unit, 'What is Contemporary?', there is a choice of two further workshop units from the following

- scriptwriting ■ novel ■ short story ■ literary editing
- poetry ■ the writer as teacher ■ critical issues.

Under individual supervision, MA students complete a full-length work, whether a novel, a collection of poems or short stories, a full-length play, TV or radio script, or a substantial editing project.

The course will suit prospective and practising writers and editors who would welcome the opportunity to work in a professional environment towards the production of substantial finished work.

For further details and an application form, please write to David Kelly Administrator
MA in Writing School of Cultural Studies
Sheffield Hallam University
Collegiate Crescent Campus Sheffield S10 2BP

Telephone 0114 225 4408

Fax 0114 225 4363

Details and application forms are also available on the Internet at www.shu.ac.uk/schools/cs/english/mawrit.htm

Teaching staff include ■ Lynne Alexander (novelist)
■ Lesley Glaister (novelist) ■ Mike Harris (playwright)
■ E A Markham (poet and editor)
■ Livi Michael (novelist) ■ Sean O'Brien (poet)
■ Jane Rogers (novelist)

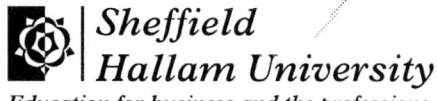

Sheffield Hallam University
Education for business and the professions

JANE HOLLAND
THE BIRTH OF THE MEDICINE MAN

Nobody knows how, but I sprang
fully-formed from a hole
in the ground: steam accompanied me
and stone shook
with its legs drawn up
as I was squeezed like toothpaste
out of that great darkness.

Once I started to live
it was seen I had an extra rib
the width of a finger.
But this is not all.
My heart, stomach and liver
were found to be crystal.

When I was old enough to dream
I began to remember
and shot bullets of quartz crystal
after me. One entered
the white space of my head
and spoke to me.
                              It said
"Fall to the ground, fall down
and let the river run over you".

So I fell and the fathomless river
ran over and around me. Fish
drummed their heels
on the thin skin of my ankles.
Earth cluttered itself
with the debris of expectation.

Strange hands reached down
and dragged me up
like a salmon caught in a net,
their long fingers
strands of shining constellations.

When I emerged
I could breathe fire and see
inside solid objects.

I saw a spirit trapped
in the mountain rocks.
I heard its voice
in the mouth of a cave.
It said "All things have their story".

Listen to the four winds.
All things have their story.

TONY ROBERTS
A FICTION OF FATHER

He'd been papering Occupied France
with 'The Courrier de l'Air': "a jaunt".
Tumbling illustrated booklets over
Rouen when flak exploded in their face,
the orange bursting in the white. Out went
the radio; the compass jammed, leaving
my navigator Father dispossessed
of those routines that calmed him down. Snafu.

Dead reckoning coming home. He watched
the Channel, stiff as wavy, brylcreemed hair,
through shredded linen on the fuselage.
Engines clattered; night chattered; Father mouthed
wet smoke and vomit, methyl bromide fumes.

I recreate this from buff envelopes
of his war service: letters, clippings, stubs
and passes, photos, "gen". Here, for instance,
is the demob diary in which Father
plotted only train departures, gifts he'd sent,
and coded states of mind – "Stockings. Preston.
6 and H". Three years of war had taught him
disappointment is expectation's twin.

Tomorrow I will put him on his train,
illuminate the carriage, frame his mood.
But for tonight he flies his Wellington
on that fainting July night in '43:
freezing, feral, fumbling and flak-blind,
a father lost this month – by his lost son.

PETER REDGROVE
WATCHING THE VENTIFACTS

The smooth grooves
            and flutings of ventifacts,
                        the water slate dark,

The wind blows off the water
            with its verb:
                        stand up, kneel down, open this,

Look at that; what the wind says
        to do, must be done.
                      We were sealed in

Because the wind
            could not shake the storms
                        out of the huge cloudbanks:

Then it did, and the whole world poured
        in black masses
                      like the entrails

Of coalmines streaked with all minerals;
        weather that puts you in a trance
                  with its smooth-gliding

Coal-black machinery
        then plucks you out of it
                  with a relenting breeze –

Can listen to a breeze talking
        for hours moving about
                  like another person in the house

Opening and shutting doors;
        then more clouds sail
                  out of the promontory

And carry me away, or leave me
        looking up into the sky, where I can watch
                The planet breathing.

JOHN HARTLEY WILLIAMS
HOT FIVE
i.m. Louis Armstrong

"Gentlemen, the wax is hot and you may play".
The clarinet swoops, the guitarist, with a fan of fingers,
                              plays a chord,
cornet and trombone start a dirty quarrel
about which way to play the melody.

The leading hornman's first arpeggio
ravishes the scale, then with full vibrato
                              skies a note
and holds it. The critic, taking pulse, feels
his pressure start a heady rise.

The trombone burps and blathers,
seesaws fatly, riding up
                 like some stout citizen
loose inside an urchin's playground,
then down.

The clarinet's a seagull
following a ferry. Poised upon an updraught,
                              it floats astern,
then wheels between the smokestacks,
crying out.

They play with a bottle of Miss Urzey's gin
open on the table. The guitarist,
                 with his legs crossed,
is leaning over his instrument. It looks
as if he's pulling something from his entrails.

The critic notes they've made it up –
or most of it – as they progress. He takes
                              a fluffed note
for "the drastic nature of an inspiration".
A collision on that fill-in – it sends

"a frisson of delight along your leg" the way
perfection never could. A chair in the studio
                              falls over, faithfully recorded.

The main man soars across its bump. Somebody
is laughing, shouting, as the next solo ignites.

Twenty eight years later, in an attic, a boy
winds the handle of an ancient gramophone,
                      opens wide its loudness doors
and puts a fat brass needle in the pick up
(for the full impact of modern sound reproduction).

"What is the source of this music's power?
Social repression? Naivete? Or does it just express
                      the joy of being alive?"
The critic is genuinely puzzled. He writes: "perhaps
it was a moment when art and popularity coincided".

In the attic, trombone, clarinet and cornet
storm towards the end of their three minutes:
                      "the final *rapprochement*
of that polyphonic ride-out lifts us into a new dimension".
Quite. And the needle scratches on the playout groove.

MERRYN WILLIAMS

A SISTER RECALLS

My brother had a quiet voice; you had to strain
to hear him from the back of a crowded room.

My brother spoke in the debate on conscription, said
he'd always be last to go forth and the first to retreat.

When the newspapers cried, "Young men, march forward!"
he sat in one place and smiled, 'I'm a coward'.

He liked chess problems, hiking above the snow;
should have been a girl because girls didn't go.

My brother was lost in the summer advance;
his name is written on blue glass

in the college chapel. They dedicated
the window before the Lord Lieutenant

and other dignitaries, swathed in black.
I went there and looked once. I shan't go back.

HUGH MacPHERSON
RUE DES SOLITAIRES

Really there are several streets, of course –
standing in one place it's true but
what you see on a slow day of summer
is never remotely the same as the distant
busily engaged street of a day of rain,
or the frigid nod of acquaintance
that's all even familiar buildings will give you
in the early hours of autumn.

The fig trees and the passageways are
as much as you can count on, but even they,
like cats, if you stay away too long
will specialise in that deliberate
self-conscious gaze in another direction,
only to be broken by careful cultivation:
a clear admission on your part
that separation has hurt you too.

But early on a summer morning,
as your hands anticipate the warmth
of bread and the window sill whose brick
is fiercely hot by noon, the fig trees lean far out
into the street – with their milk-sweet breath
and a leaf just touching briefly on your shoulder,
as you pass by on the way through
the city's sunstarred canyons.

It trains you either way finally –
the rue des Solitaires. How to get by alone,
if you must, with its garrulously changing
stones and vegetation that provide the roots
of conversation for those who climb from the square
each day – to survive on the bare ritual of
weather words with the corner shop and baker
(except Monday early closing – a time of silence).

Or to be ready for the changeability of lives
shared too closely – teaching that the angry sigh,
– or jealousy, affection, rage – are not definitive
reactions but part of a whole democracy of love:

where emotions vote in shifting conspiracy
of responses to what we are or said or didn't do or
should have thought of. While the aftermath, made curiously
strong, enjoys the contrast with what went before.

TONY CURTIS
AT THE WATER'S EDGE

After the swordplay with his walking stick,
after the calendar collapsed,
after the garage was locked and the car
driven away by his son,
long after the smutty asides, the accusations
that his wife of sixty years was seeing
the head of Physics long dead,
shortly after the raged throwing of the tea set,
the two-year long sleepy day ending.
Interference. The pictures fuzzy and fading.

He remembers rising from the settee
to stand for the Queen;
one of the school field smokers he caned,
who became a Professor of Law;
and a pretty, young teacher of cookery.
From his armchair in the Water's Edge
he can see the Channel and the Somerset hills.
The tanker like a painted ship
waiting for the tide, or the fall of night
when its waste can be leaked into the sea.

The National Poetry Competition 1999

The 1999 National Poetry Competition, sponsored by BT (First Prize £5000), was judged by John Agard, Robert Crawford, and Ruth Padel, with Michael Rosen in the Chair.

First Prize

SIMON RAE
BELIEVED

There's a missing person in everyone,
a draft-dodger, truant, man-on-the-run,

deserter, defaulter, garden-fence-vaulter,
an into-the-wide-blue-yonder absconder,

and I found mine, or he found me,
and together we sauntered out for a paper

or a carton of milk that wasn't needed
to match the one that would turn to cheese

while the cheese beside it turned slowly green,
leaving the bed unmade and the garden unseeded

and a bit of a mystery to explain.
The wagging tongues went worrying back

to the gap in the hedge and the hole in the fence
and to how they'd somehow always suspected

there was more to the case than met the eye
and if only they'd known as they walked the dog

or pushed the buggy round the block
that that was the definitive last Good Evening

it would have been easier making sense
of what they now saw was a chain of events...

Meanwhile smoke-rings float to the ceiling
prompting this out-of-body sensation

that I'm looking down on a pile of clothing
artistically folded there on the shingle

and thinking how I'd left my life
like a field of snow which a confident witness

would swear blind he'd seen me cross,
yet find, when he came to prove his point,

no tracks to show in the unblemished whiteness...

Second Prize

ENDA WYLEY
DIARY OF A FATMAN

I am so fat now
that the woman I love
will not lie down with me –
so I make her shape in the mountains
of potatoes I boil and mash,
feel her breasts in the dough I knead and prick,
her bread nipples rising erect at 200 degrees Celsius,
hear her noises gurgling with the bubbling
of tomato, ginger, cinnamon,
her kisses extra sweetness oozing.
Skin, heaped spoons of creme fraiche,
eyes, sharp kiwi green,
mouth, a dazzling lemon split apart –

I am so fat now
she is all of this to me and more.
I make my bed in the sitting room,
unable to climb the stairs.
I sleep with my heavy boots on,
unable to pull them off.
Sometimes she passes by my door –
the dart of a thin shadow,
her breasts suddenly shrivelled
as an avocado's outer layer,
her skin rough like uncooked rice,
her eyes two empty plates pleading,
I look at you and can never eat again.

Her voice has the rancid stench
of food left over for weeks.
She is becoming nothing –
ice-cream melted on a hot kitchen floor,
boiled water evaporating in a room.
But I make her again – my woman.
Her love among the carrots, onions and garlic
is so heated in my thick, tasty stew
that I do not notice her open the front door
then leave the house for good –
the smell of food a jaded world forever clinging
to her hair, her skin and clothes.
Not hearing, I scoop, scoop from my pot
into the biggest bowl I can find.

THIRD PRIZE
SUE HUBBARD
GHOST STATION: ROSSLYN

Wild garlic and rain in the woods and between invisible tracks
that lead from here to there I sense them glide
through their lost narratives down platforms of damp ferns.

Think of a bent hair-pin lodged for years under a wooden carriage seat
fallen from a stook of auburn hair, a single collar-stud trapped beneath
the floor that once fastened small intimacies behind a film of beaded glass,

or an old man's knotted hand, knuckles raw in the niche of his lap
carrying home a gift of speckled eggs. Imagine the pallor of rain:
ashen, pewter, stained watery-sheen along a backbone of glinting steel,

and shadows of coal-dust, steam and sparks on iron where green tongues
of larkspur grow. Turn your head and glimpse between verticals of larch
and beech blotched autobiographies like smudged footprints in wet grass.

Listen, where the wind throws back its dialogue of despair behind
the raindrops, acknowledging lives drained away, like a plume
of smoke recalled along invisible tracks by a damp bird's solitary song.

NEWS/COMMENT

POETRY INTERNATIONAL

Every two years the October Poetry Fest extends to a week with Poetry International at the South Bank, prolonging poetry awareness beyond The Day. The format is well established by now: international must-sees such as Mahmoud Darwish, Yehuda Amichai, Yves Bonnefoy, Kamau Brathwaite, the local staples, James Fenton, Carol Ann Duffy, Don Paterson, the hot new international name (new to us that is) Billy Collins; many hands reworking a classic: this time it's Dante, with versions from Michael Longley, Jamie McKendrick, Ciaran Carson, Fleur Adcock, Lavinia Greenlaw et al. Innovations include Anthony Minghella talking about poetry and film and Tom Philllips on Dante.

Poetry International runs from Friday, October 6th, the day after National Poetry Day, to Saturday October 14th. Box Office: 020 7960 4242

NET VERSE

Frank Parker's site at http://www.mbay.net/~faparker/ contains samples not only of his own work but also that of several other excellent poets. Jim Wilson's minimalist poems, and those of Michael Rothenberg particularly appealed to me. A recent and very welcome addition is a set of translations of Jacques Prévert by Anne Berkeley. To anyone who knows Prévert only through Ferlinghetti's aged and rather stolid renditions, these versions will come as a breath of fresh air. That Parker is in California, while Berkeley lives in Cambridge, UK, is another example of how the Internet renders geography largely irrelevant. Similarly, Farrago Poetry organises poetry events in the UK, and has a particular fondness for poetry slams. But their suitably lively site at http://www.e-poets.net/Farrago/ is actually hosted by the e-poets network in Chicago. Check it out for details of their latest promotions. The parent site at http://www.e-poets.net is also worth a visit while you're in the vicinity.

TextWorx Toolshed at http://www.burningpress.org/toolbox/index.html is the place to go if you're looking for software kick-start your creativity. Here you'll find Mac and PC programs that will generate stories, randomise words, and otherwise re-organise and re-assemble language. There should be something here for any experimentalist writer who wants new ways to mangle text. If you prefer your poetry a little less frenzied, you could do worse that saunter over to *Ixion* at http://www.btinternet.com/~ixionmag/ where you'll find an eclectic selection of poems, prose, artwork and cartoons. When I visited, it had work by John Horváth and Lawrence Sail, amongst others.

Another stylish new magazine comes from the people who brought you *Tears in the Fence*. It's called *Wandering Dog* and you can find its elegantly presented poetry and prose at http://www.wanderingdog.co.uk/

If you wander across any other good sites, let me know about them at peter@hphoward.demon.co.uk

LETTERS

POETS WITH HANDLES

Dear Mr Forbes,

A couple of points about William Scammell's review of The Oxford Book of English Verse.

The first is bound to matter more to me than to others, including him, but the "eighty-page essay on Geoffrey Hill's use of hyphens (collected in *The Force of Poetry*)" has thirty-seven pages. (There are two distinct essays on Hill.) Maybe I exaggerated the interest of hyphenation, not only in itself (though the great language-man Eric Partridge knew how much might turn on so small a thing), but in Hill, and in the many other poets who figure in that essay: Samuel Daniel, Coleridge, Tennyson, Hopkins, Dickinson, Yeats, and Eliot. But Mr Scammell adds his own exaggeration, doubling up in merriment.

The second point may be of more general interest: his complaining that poets are accorded by me their social titles.

> Betjeman and Empson get handles stuck on to them on the Contents page: Sir John, Sir William, etc. In which case why not "Ted Hughes OM" and "Joe Bloggs OBE"? Grigson pointed out long ago that this sort of pomp is utterly out of place in poetry [and so on].

As it happens, I had at first wondered whether to follow the traditional practice of giving such titles.

But a moment's thought brought home that there would be a high price to be paid for not doing so. Would Mr Scammell really want readers to meet only John Wilmot, with no indication that he is better-known as the Earl of Rochester? Henry Howard, no Earl of Surrey? James Graham, no Marquis of Montrose? George Granville, no Lord Lansdowne? Anne Finch, no Countess of Winchilsea? Mary Herbert, no Countess of Pembroke?

All of these poets, and others who inevitably raise problems of nomenclature are to be found in *The Oxford Book of English Verse*. Both forms of their names are given, so as to be helpful, in the index of poets. It is true that Betjeman and Empson would present no obstacle to a searcher or a reader, but I trust that Mr Scammell would not be content were Betjeman and Empson (and Wyatt and Sidney) to be stripped of their knighthoods while Surrey and Rochester and the Countess of Winchilsea were allowed to retain their classier titles. An anthologist may judge that not putting needless obstacles in the way of readers is more responsible, and more politically decent, than any flushed unthinking populism.

I even think it proper to have recorded that Robert Southwell, unlike Mr Scammell and me, is a Saint.

Yours sincerely,
CHRISTOPHER RICKS
Boston University

GROVE OFFENCES

Dear Peter,

I'm pleased Paul Groves found much to enjoy in our selection for *The Forward Book of Poetry*, reviewed in *Poetry Review* (Vol 89 No 4, p.63), in which his own fine poem appears.

I'm surprised, however, he's unaware that Carol Ann Duffy's poem 'The Devil's Wife' is told in the voice of a Myra Hindley/Rosemary West, as Carol Rumens notes in her review (p. 33) of *The World's Wife*. Hard to see how this went unnoticed. A clear case here of the need to focus on the poem not on the poet?

This also applies to 'horse under water' by Caroline Carver. I don't accept the reviewer's suggestion that the poet appropriates the culture of an ethnic minority. Her poem is rooted in her West Indian childhood and is a richly empathetic piece brimming with delight in and respect for the place and its vital living patois.

Sophie Hannah's poem 'Next Door Despised' hardly deserves to be dismissed as "nonsense". Her technically and emotionally accomplished poem pushes sense to its boundary, redefining logic with her tenacious wit.

And of course the aresehole, cunt, etc in Andrew Motion's poem 'Serenade' are equine, belonging to the eponymous horse.

Yours sincerely,
PENELOPE SHUTTLE
Falmouth
Cornwall

PBS EXCLUSIVE BOOK SUPPLY SERVICE

Readers of *Poetry Review* can receive the UK-published books featured in the magazine post-free from the Poetry Book Society. If your local bookshop's idea of a poetry section is a shelf of Keats *Collected* and two tatty copies of *The Waste Land* this is what you've been waiting for! Call 020 8870 8403 between 9.30am and 5.30pm Mon-Fri to make your order, quoting "*Poetry Review*". All major credit/debit cards accepted, including Switch.

THE SOCIETY OF AUTHORS

Eric Gregory Awards 2001

Annual awards totalling up to £24,000 for the encouragement of young poets.

A candidate must be British by birth, under the age of 30, and may submit a published or unpublished volume of poetry
(up to 30 poems).

Closing date 31 October 2000.

Full details and entry form from:
Awards Secretary, The Society of Authors, 84 Drayton Gardens, London SW10 9SB.
Please send SAE.

ENDSTOPS

HUM

Dear Sir,

Much as I enjoyed the Tobias Hill poem ('The Lighthouse Keeper's Cat') in your spring 2000 issue (Vol 90 No 1, p.34), it was spoilt for me by the line "the hummingbirds greener than green".

The quotation which headed the poems suggested that this poems was set in New Zealand and hummingbirds have never existed there. I think such background research is important if a poem gives the impression of a historical and geographical setting.

Yours sincerely,
DAVID HOWARD
Wiltshire

A LEAF OUT OF HIS BOOK

Dear Peter Forbes,

Penelope Shuttle's *A Leaf Out Of His Book* runs to 83 poems over 147 pages. Whatever its merits, it deserves more than just to serve as a footnote to one of John Burnside's name-dropping essays (Gary Snyder, Paul Virilio, Magritte, Proust, Heidegger) on poetry, masquerading as a review (Vol 90 No 1, p.79). Perhaps it's because I'd been spoilt by reading all the proper reviews written by all the other male reviewers (a bit light on women reviewers this issue. Carol Rumens stuck out), that I was so disappointed. If John Burnside wants to show off the breadth of his reading and erudition, and hypothecate on the metaphysics of poetry, could he please save it for an essay in, say, *PNR*? I promise I'd read it: what he said was interesting, and I was with him all the way.

Yours sincerely
ROSALIND EYRE
Leicester

SOME CONTRIBUTORS

Moniza Alvi's new collection, *Carrying My Wife*, is forthcoming from Bloodaxe,

Mary Jo Bang's poems here come from a MS called *Louise in Love* to be published in January 2001 by Grove Press.

David Berman has released three lps with his rock band the Silver Jews.

Stephen Burt is a Graduate student at Yale.

Kate Clanchy's latest collection is *Samarkand* (Chatto).

Jeff Clark's first book, *The Little Door Slides Back*, won the National Poetry Series Award and was published by Sun & Moon Press in 1998.

Robert Crawford's *The New Penguin Book of Scottish Verse* (co-edited with Mick Imlah) is due from Penguin in the Autumn.

Tom French (b. 1965) lives in Dublin, and will shortly publish his first collection with Gallery Press. He works as a librarian.

Mark Halliday runs the Creative Writing Program at the University of Ohio.

Brian Henry teaches at the University of Georgia; he is an editor of *Verse*.

Ellen Hinsey's first collection *Cities of Memory* won the Yale Younger Poets Series Award. The poems here come form a new book-length sequence *Vita Contemplativa*.

John Kinsella's latest collection is *The Visitants* (Bloodaxe).

August Kleinzahler's *Live From the Hong Kong Nile Club* is due from Faber in September.

Hugh Macpherson was shortlisted for the Geoffrey Dearmer Prize in 1999.

Jules Mann's pamphlet *Pluck* was publisher by Slow Dancer in 1999.

Malinda Markham teaches at Tokyo University.

Dennis O'Driscoll's latest collection is *Weather Permitting* (Anvil).

Andrew Osborn teaches at the University of Texas.

Justin Quinn's second collection, *Privacy*, was published by Carcanet in 1999. With David Wheatley he is an editor of *Metre* and teaches at Charles University, Prague.

Claudia Rankine's latest collection is *The End of the Alphabet* (Grove Press, 1998).

Tracy Ryan's first collection in the UK, *The Willing Eye*, was published by Bloodaxe in 1999.

Caitriona O'Reilly's first collection *The Nowhere Birds* is due next year from Bloodaxe.

Philip Salom won the 1987 Commonwealth Poetry Prize.

Carole Satyamurti's latest collection is *Love and Variations* (Bloodaxe).

Adam Schwartzman's latest collection is *(Merrie) Afrika!* (Carcanet).

John Stammers' first collection, *Panoramic Lounge-bar,* will be published by Picador in January 2001.

Kathleen Stewart was born in Sydney in 1958. She has published 6 novels and two collections of poetry, the latest being *The White Star* (Minerva Australia, 1997).

Stephen Troussé is the editor of *papercuts* magazine and plays guitar and sings with the Foxgloves.

James Tate's *Selected Poems* are published by Carcanet.

Karen Volkman's first collection, *Crash's Law* (Norton) was reviewed in *PR* Vol 88 No 1, 1998.

István Vörös lives in Budapest, and is one of Hungary's most widely-published young poets.

Sarah Wardle won the 1999 Geoffrey Dearmer Prize.

David Wheatley's first collection, *Thirst*, was published by Gallery. He is an editor of *Metre*.

Jane Yeh lives in New York, where she works for *Village Voice* magazine. Her poems have appeared in *Boston Review*, *Metre* and elsewhere.

Monica Youn is Wallace Stegner Fellow in Poetry at Stanford University. She was published in *New Poetries 2* (Carcanet).